# The Pastor's Paradox

Serving God and Burning Out

DR. BYRON WASHINGTON

# Dedication

This book is dedicated to every pastor and leader who has answered the sacred call to shepherd God's people and advance His Kingdom. Ministry is a paradox—both exhausting and exhilarating, weighty and wondrous, burdensome and deeply meaningful—all at once. It is for those who labor faithfully in the unseen places, who give even when weary, who lead while quietly teetering on the edge of burnout.

To you who carry the mantle of leadership with both trembling and courage: thank you. Your sacrifice, your prayers, your sleepless nights, and your steadfast commitment are invaluable to the Kingdom. May you be reminded that your work is not in vain, and that even in the weariness, God is building something eternal through you.

# CONTENTS

# PREFACE

HELP. The idea of "help" is not always straightforward. Have you ever offered help to somebody who you knew needed help but they rejected your offer? Have you ever attempted to help somebody, and they wanted to tell you the best way to help them, but their instructions only worsened the situation? Help is complex because it can be interpreted in many ways. The person offering it is (hopefully) doing it out of care or concern. The receiver may see it as the person taking pity on them, judging them, or determining that the receiver is powerless to complete the task. We all need help, though we do not always realize the help we truly need.

In the book of Acts, there is a story about a man who is laid daily at the temple gate to beg alms. He was begging because he was paralyzed and unable to use his legs. Peter and John approach the temple gate, and the paralyzed man thinks he will receive money from them. Peter gives him much more, but in reality, Peter gives him what he needs. The man did not need the money. He needed his legs. If he regained movement in his legs, he could earn a living and not beg.

Our world promotes self-help, which is not bad, but what happens when you cannot help yourself and nobody around you seems to care? Have you ever helped someone else, and when you needed help, there was no one around, and you were forced to try to help yourself? That is the story of many pastors pouring out and giving their best to the congregation, yet when they need help, no one helps them. This book is meant to help pastors because the terrain of ministry has become treacherous, yet pastors are still willing to stand in the trenches and declare truth, hope, and love.

If you have a child or have been around children, there are moments when they call for help. Sometimes, they need help. Other times, they need guidance to navigate the situation. A child's request for help can often be void of information, so as a parent or adult, you will have to ask the child what they need so that you know how to proceed. As adults, receiving help takes on a different shade. We may not know who to speak with, and asking for help can create stigmas or hamper our professional progression, depending on the nature of the intervention.

Even when we know help is needed, we do not always administer (or receive) it correctly. Pastors need help. Pastors need help not because they cannot lead the flock of God but because the topography of the church environment has changed so rapidly over the years. They need assistance from people who are not necessarily at ground zero with them but who have a higher vantage point and can point out pitfalls and valleys before pastors fall in and endanger their lives.

Help is best rendered at the beginning or the onset of an issue. Before you go any further, take a minute to think about where you are in your pastoral journey. When you started, are you where you'd imagine you would be? How has ministry changed for you over the last five years? What are you hoping for and looking for God to do in the next season of your ministry? If you are experiencing burnout, your ministry future can become blurry and obstructed. Whether you have been in ministry for two or 32 years, take a moment to slow down and think about what is about to be shared. From research to the personal testimony of pastors, find yourself in this book and take this journey as we explore this paradox.

For by wise counsel you
can wage your war, and in
an abundance of
counselors there is
victory and safety.

— Proverbs 24:6 (AMPC)

# Introduction

Pastors and burnout. Although my doctoral dissertation ultimately focused on this topic, it was not where I initially intended to begin or wanted my research to go. Burnout interested me, though I wanted to examine burnout in physicians. Then, in the middle of one of my early semesters, I decided to focus on something more relevant or pressing in our current society. So, I started working in a different direction and even wrote a paper for one of my classes on "Food Deserts." Food deserts are urban areas that are void of proper grocery stores. I thought this would be fascinating, and as I started the research, it was indeed interesting.

Nevertheless, I did not feel excited about it. Continuing the process of trying to decide what I was going to focus on for my dissertation, I stopped and prayed. Prayer should have probably been my first stop on this journey. God does not always speak, but He does *speak*. I hope that makes sense. I went back to burnout and physicians. Then He started speaking. I saw article after article about pastors burning out. I got the hint, and when I looked at pastoral burnout, I realized that is where God wanted me to focus.

I explain the journey because I believe this book and all the research are God-directed to help pastors. Pastors are essential in the development and growth of the church. If pastors are not functioning at optimal cognitive capacity, they will be limited in their ability to help grow and develop the Body of Christ. The part of burnout that puzzled me was how pastors who are connected to the Almighty God were seemingly powerless against burnout. They were preaching about the Light of the World, yet their light was waxing dim. This puzzle is the paradox that we explore in this book. In the final portions of editing this book, I saw and continue to see countless articles online about burnout, social media posts from pastors talking about the burden of pastoring, and people who decided to leave ministry for various reasons related to burnout.

In all honesty, you could read this book just for the solutions, though I implore you to sit with the topics discussed, wrestle with the concepts provided, and work through the examples in the book. This book does not tell you or any pastor how to pastor. It is a guide to help make sure that pastors "fight a good fight, finish their course, and keep the faith." When I was growing up attending our annual conference, when it was time for the preacher of the hour to stand up to preach, the Presiding Elder would implore everyone to "gather at their tent door," a reference to the Old Testament and the children of Israel as they worshipped God in the wilderness.

I encourage you to do the same. God is speaking to us and guiding us on how not to burn out as pastors or how to support our pastors so they can do all God calls them to do. The writer of Proverbs continually admonishes us that wisdom and understanding are keys too essential to ignore, "How much better to get wisdom than gold! To get understanding is to be chosen rather than silver." (Proverbs 16:16 ESV).

The sad reality is this: you could skip through the book, get a few solutions, and say you know everything. However, let me ask you this: would you want a pilot who skimmed over the emergency flight manual or one who took it seriously? Every pastor may not burn out, nor will every pilot have to face a flight emergency, but woe to the pilot who encounters an emergency and is not prepared or to the pastor who is burning out and has no guidance for combating burnout.

This book contains years of research compressed into a readable form for pastors and church leaders. I pray you read it with grace and an open heart, allowing God's spirit to speak to you. I am writing alongside you to assist and equip you with all you need to fight our common enemy. So that you, as the leader of your church, can continue to change lives and not be constrained by burnout. If you are a pastor who is burned out, may this book assure you that all is not lost, and your hope will not be cut off.

God Bless and Always Be Encouraged,
Byron Washington, Ed. D

---

"Burnout is a gateway
used by the enemy to gain
access to pastors with the
intent of damaging,
derailing and destroying
their ministry."

– Dr. Byron Washington

---

# 1

# THE GATEWAY TO BURNOUT

"You should be having a stroke at this moment. I thought it was only asthma. What is going on? I want to quit. This calling is too much. I never even wanted to be a pastor. What should I do? This meeting was not on my schedule. My family is suffering. My health has declined. I am doing my best. I am only one person. Is it me, God, or the enemy?" These are statements, questions, or thoughts that many pastors have asked and are pondering even as they read this book. The feelings and thoughts mentioned above are not randomly generated. Those thoughts were voiced by actual pastors who have faced and encountered burnout, many of whom you will hear from as we journey through this book. Pastoral comments of this nature are often directly or indirectly linked to burnout. In the life of a pastor, burnout becomes the gateway to other issues, concerns, or vices.

In many places around the world, when you enter a country's capital, they have a city gate. The city gate is usually a large structure that lets you know you are now entering a specific territory. When a pastor feels burned out, they are approaching the city gate. They are approaching the territory of burnout, and if they enter, the way out is not a simple U-turn. To get out of burnout usually requires a series of turns, stops, and roundabouts to start heading in the right direction. The scary reality is that, unlike the gate at the entrance to a big city, the entrance into burnout is not as visible. However, once a person enters that territory, the effect on their life and ministry is unmistakable.

The underlying conversation is not about city gates; it is about access. When burnout has access to our lives, it opens the door for many other issues to enter. Burnout is often the beginning of a more significant set of problems if not addressed immediately. The use of narcotics is a practical example of this phenomenon.

In conversations about drugs and chemical dependency, certain drugs are historically considered gateway drugs. Research suggests that these drugs can potentially lead a person to try more powerful or addictive drugs. The United States National Institutes of Health conducted a study and found that nicotine primes the brain to enhance cocaine's effects. [1]

> For pastors, burnout has become the enemy's gateway "drug" of choice.

Nicotine, in this example, is a gateway drug. It does not mean that every person who smokes cigarettes will use cocaine. However, depending on the person's condition, experience, or environment, these drugs open the door and can lead a person into a place far worse than where they started. For pastors, burnout has become the enemy's "gateway drug" of choice. Let us examine why.

## Hidden in Plain Sight

First, burnout is subtle. Burnout does not aggressively grab a pastor in attempts to hijack their ministry. If we use a car to symbolize the pastor's ministry, burnout rides quietly, first in the backseat, then creeps to the passenger seat. Eventually, burnout is driving, and the person is going for a ride they did not request. Burnout can and often happens out in the open. Burnout is not behind closed doors; it is not secret text messages or hidden addictions (though these things can be a byproduct of burnout). A pastor can be in church serving, faithful, committed, and burning out in front of their family, friends, and congregation. A pastor can provide the most potent series on hope and the power of God and internally feel hopeless and powerless. This state is the paradox that we will explore.

Second, burnout is not directly listed as a sin. A pastor cannot expressly open their Bible and point to burnout, though there are some examples that people often refer to related to burnout (think Moses and Elijah). It is not adultery or fornication; it is not lying or stealing. The Apostle Paul does not list it in his letters to churches in the New Testament, nor does God write it on the stone tablets Moses brought down off the mountain. In 2 Timothy 4, The Apostle Paul admonishes Timothy to be instant "in season and out of season." For some pastors, "to be instant in season and out of season" means pushing even when your body is yearning for a break. I would suggest this is not how Paul intended this statement to be interpreted. For pastors, burnout can act as a charlatan, masking itself in various ways. This "masking" creates a conundrum for pastors who constantly ask, "is this me, is this God, or is this the enemy?"

Is this me because I want a vacation, God because he knows I need rest, or is this the enemy trying to lull me into a place of complacency? Almost every Christian has had this conversation, and this line of reasoning weighs even more heavily on pastors. Additionally, people have historically explained burnout inaccurately, leading to wrong assumptions and solutions. We must always be mindful to "ask the right questions." The enemy uses burnout because people ask the wrong questions or use an inaccurate description of burnout. The enemy using this tactic intends to keep leaders blind to his effects, all the while parading his schemes in front of us.

Consider this: we often hear the word "stress" to describe burnout. However, a person can be stressed and not burned out. Read that again; a pastor can be experiencing stress and not be burned out. For example, in preparation for a large conference or special event, the pastor, staff, and members work for months planning and organizing the event. They may be stressed, but they are not technically burned out. Why? Because when that event is over, that added stress is gone. Burnout does not evaporate that quickly.

Burnout is an ideal tool because the enemy knows that many leaders are reluctant to admit their current condition. Varying factors can cause this reluctance. So even when they feel burned out because they are working for God, many will continue to "go forward" even when no gas is in the tank. We all know pastors who have "pushed" the "car of ministry" with no gas in the tank and still declared they were okay; my friends, this is not faith, and it is not helpful. A few months ago, a pastor spoke about a period early in their ministry when they had a full preaching, teaching, and counseling schedule. He was "working for God" and found himself burned out. He believed he was the only one who could do what he was doing. He believed his physical body would continue to run on faith, fasting, the Holy Spirit, minimal sleep, and prayer.

One day, he was at a catholic church for a community meeting; he was tired and thinking about his next appointment. He happened to look up at the crucifix that was in the sanctuary. At that moment, he realized he had not died on the cross; he was not the "only" person who could change lives, and saving *everyone* was not his responsibility. He concluded that he was trying to be Jesus, though not intentionally. He realized his humanity and changed his approach to ministry and pastoring.

If pastors are not constantly running, pushing, pressing, and exerting themselves to the highest level, somehow, people think they are not doing their best for God. This mindset is not the pastor's fault. It is a combination of the fast-paced world we live in, people's expectations, and the changing dynamics of ministry. A pastor can love God and their congregation, have boundaries, get decent sleep, and have peace and rest.

Those ideals are not sinful; they are necessary and not mutually exclusive.

As we continue discussing burnout, we will refer to these areas because they are the keys to addressing burnout as it relates to pastors. As we will discuss later, burnout happens over time, but it is essential to know what it is and is not.

To enhance and provide additional context for pastoral burnout, we will hear stories and examples from nine pastors about their experiences with burnout. Pseudonyms have been used for confidentiality; however, these pastors have provided candid thoughts, experiences, and observations on burnout. During these interviews, there were some heavy moments and moments of joy when we understood the mercy of God and his ever-present grace. These pastors' stories and experiences remind us that pastors are human. Their hearts and minds face the same restrictions as every other human, and the result can be catastrophic when we press our bodies beyond their capacity. This book is not a critique but a conversation and a starting point for the church to unpack and reevaluate how we handle our pastors.

Again, this book is not a critique of pastors. The book examines the patterns, actions, and activities that pastors engage in and how those areas can lead to burnout if not appropriately managed. Pastors are an essential part of our world and, practically speaking, are a large part of our labor force. [2]Their job as a spiritual leader is *strenuous and joyous, painful and pleasant, and lonely and loving all at the same time.*

> [The job of] a spiritual leader is strenuous and joyous, painful and pleasant, and lonely and loving all at the same time.

The pastor's paradox is the quandary of serving God, being on fire for Him, yet feeling your light going dim and burning out. The end of this book provides some practical ways to address and mitigate burnout, but the real focus is on understanding and wisdom. "Wisdom is the principal thing; therefore get wisdom: and with all, thy getting get understanding (Proverbs 4:7 KJV).

These pastors were willing to share their thoughts, personal stories, and insights about their encounters. Their transparency helps every pastor know that they are seen and heard and that every pastor may face difficult decisions at some point. Burnout is the concern that even if a pastor has not personally experienced it, they know of a colleague or have heard about a pastor who was a victim of burnout.

We will journey with and hear from our nine pastors as we discuss burnout. Much of the research contained in this book comes from my doctoral research and dissertation.[3]

*Pastoral Demographics*

| Participant | Years as a Pastor | Congregation Size | Location | Education | Financial Support |
| --- | --- | --- | --- | --- | --- |
| Pastor Jessica | 30 | More Than 100 | Urban | Doctorate | Full time |
| Pastor Daniel | 24 | 101-250 | Urban | Doctorate | Bi-vocational |
| Pastor Esther | 20 | 50 or less | Urban | Bachelors | Bi-vocational |
| Pastor Ryan | 9 | 101-250 | Urban | Doctorate | Bi-vocational |
| Pastor Moses | 4 | 50 or less | Urban | Bachelors | Bi-vocational |
| Pastor Conner | 8 | 251-1000 | Urban | Bachelors | Bi-vocational |
| Pastor Michael | 32 | 50 or less | Suburban | Masters | Full time |
| Pastor Julius | 5 | 50 or less | Urban | Bachelors | Bi-vocational |
| Pastor Nathan | 2 | 251-1000 | Suburban | Bachelors | Full time |

The chart provides readers with a visual of the environment and dynamics of each pastor. The chart serves as an aid to assist with understanding the pastor's testimonies and stories. These pastors do not cover all aspects of demographics, but they are the starting point for our conversation. Hopefully, in the future, we can do more research and speak with more pastors about burnout. The truth is that not many pastors were willing to speak about their experiences.

It should be noted that the research was qualitative; we focused on these pastors' lived experiences. This is why the sample size is much smaller than in a quantitative or mixed-methods research approach. I hope that through this work and the additional resources that will be provided, more pastors will be willing to share and speak about their personal experiences, which assists in shedding light on how burnout affects pastors. Many pastors have been reluctant to share because those who said they had good intentions or claimed to want to help took personal information and weaponized it against those pastors.

As you will see in this book and our future endeavors, the utmost care is taken to preserve the integrity of the pastors yet share their experiences. To provide candid moments without exposing the person, their family, or congregation. The world we live in thrives off seeing people go down. People now find joy in the downfall of others, whether it be a pastor, a notable figure, or even their next-door neighbor. The enemy has made it his business to attack pastors in the city square. May this book serve as a defense and counterintelligence for positioning yourself as a pastor to win the battle against burnout. Alternatively, if you are not burning out, may this book assist in keeping you on that path. Now, let us start the conversation.

# Chapter Reflections:

1. What other books have you read on burnout as a pastor or spiritual leader, and were they helpful?

2. What other aspect of burnout would you add to the conversation about why the enemy uses it to derail and damage pastors?

3. From what position are you approaching this book?

- As a seeker (someone looking for new information, glad to learn something new, and open to new ideas)

- As a burned-out pastor (someone looking for help and answers)

- As a skeptic (someone hoping to see something "wrong" and argue that the book is not correct)

- As a support (someone who works with pastors or leaders and wants more information on the topic)

- Other

---

1. https://devtestdomain3.nih.govnews-events/nih-research-matters/why-nicotine-gateway-drug

2. Adams, C.J., Hough, H., Proeschold-bell, R.J., Yao, J., & Kolkin, M. (2017). Clergy burnout: A comparison study with other helping professions. Pastoral Psychology, 66(2), 147–175. https://doi.org/10.1007/s1108 9-016-0722-4

3. Washington, B. (2021). Understanding Burnout in Non-denominational Clergy: A Social Cognitive Approach (Doctoral dissertation, University of Southern California).

———————

Just imagine that you want to build a tower. Wouldn't you first sit down and estimate the cost to be sure you have enough to finish what you start?

— Luke 14:28 (VOICE)

The cost of a thing is the amount of what I will call life which is required to be exchanged for it, immediately or in the long run.

— Henry David Thoreau, Walden

———————

# 2

# THE COST OF CALLING

T he Bible tells us in 1 Kings 19:21 (NIV) that Elisha "took his yoke of oxen and slaughtered them. He burned the plowing equipment to cook the meat and gave it to the people, and they ate. Then he set out to follow Elijah and became his servant." Elisha left his work in the field and followed Elijah, eventually taking Elijah's place when Elijah was taken in the chariot of fire. In the New Testament, the disciples leave their work and follow Jesus.

Matthew 4:18-22 (NIV), As Jesus was walking beside the Sea of Galilee, he saw two brothers, Simon called Peter and his brother Andrew. They were casting a net into the lake, for they were fishermen. "Come, follow me," Jesus said, "and I will send you out to fish for people." At once, they left their nets and followed him. Going on from there, he saw two other brothers, James son of Zebedee, and his brother John. They were in a boat with their father, Zebedee, preparing their nets. Jesus called them, and immediately they left the boat and their father and followed him. These gentlemen were fishermen; they left their work and the family business and pivoted from fishing to becoming Jesus' disciples.

Leaving one area to follow Jesus is not an unfamiliar conversation for pastors. To follow Jesus as a pastor often requires giving up something to follow His call into ministry. The part that we do not always examine is when there is a conflict related to our calling. There are hidden costs associated with following a call.

I originally had this at the end of the book, but I felt it necessary to acknowledge that callings can be complicated. In business or life, some costs are easily seen. Then, there are hidden costs or costs that people forget to factor into the equation.

> "...it's necessary to acknowledge that callings can be complicated."

For example, when you buy a car, you can afford the payments, but have you factored in the maintenance or the cost of a new set of tires? Similarly, a pastor can be called and have conflicts (hidden or unknown costs) following that call. Though we do not have time to exhaust this conversation, almost everyone called in the Bible had some conflict related to their calling. Moses, Nehemiah, Esther, Joseph, and Paul had to address internal or external conflicts to follow their calling. There are two ways to describe calling: academic and spiritual.

The academic explanation says, "a transcendent summons, experienced as originating beyond the self, to approach a particular life role in a manner oriented toward demonstrating or deriving a sense of purpose or meaningfulness and that holds other-oriented values and goals as primary sources of motivation."[1]

The version that most of us as Christians are familiar with is "a task set by God with a sense of obligation to work for purposes other than one's own."[2] When called, we are asked to fulfill a task that is not about us. Whether in the academic or spiritual sense, the focus of the call is not on us, but on other people.

If a person is following a call, there must be a caller; in this case, it is God. So, ignoring the call becomes a challenging option. We can look to the prophet Jonah to see how ignoring God turns out. When addressing pastors, calling is central to the idea that this individual is following something they feel cannot be deviated from, though there is an understanding that callings can differ with each individual.[3] The researcher Duffy notes that in a perfect scenario, a person would understand their calling and pursue it without hindrance.[4] Duffy is correct, though we know that is not how it happens. When God calls, we must exit the highway we are on and find our way (often by the leading of the Holy Spirit) to the road that God is calling us to.

Within the context of callings, there are potholes. If you own a car, you are familiar with potholes. Potholes (honestly speaking) are not harmful when visible or if there is a sign encouraging you to exercise caution on the road. The worst potholes are the ones we do not see until it is too late. When you hit unseen potholes, you pray that your car does not lose a tire and that you have not done any extensive damage. I know this from experience. I was driving through New York, and it was raining. I was behind a tractor-trailer, and I was changing lanes to see more clearly. As I was changing lanes, I saw a pothole, but it was too late. BOOM! I knew my tire had come off, though it had not. I breathed a sigh of relief. However, as I continued to drive, I knew something was wrong. I made it home and took the car to the mechanic the next day. That pothole cost me a significant amount of money in repairs. Let's just say, unexpected potholes can be costly.

The potholes in following a calling could be avoided or even prepared for if there were signs or indications. These potholes are the activities, responsibilities, risks, issues, or concerns pastors do not realize are there until they are on the journey or, unfortunately, until they hit one. Once a pastor hits a pothole, they are quickly aware of its presence. However, the damage has already been done in many cases. Callings can challenge a person's well-being because of the physical, emotional, and physiological connection.[5] It is noted that individuals could face internal struggles and encounter "work-family imbalances, inter-role conflict, negative physical/psychological effects, and emotional labor" following a calling.[6] These effects are a reality for pastors.

I would suggest that few pastors can say that their entire pastoring journey was without some challenging and demanding moments. These conflicting actions all connect to why pastors are susceptible to burnout. These demanding moments require pastors to lean heavily on God. As we go through this discussion on burnout, the presence of the enemy (the devil, Satan) and the need to trust and lean on God may not always be directly stated, though it is implied. _Note:_ (this is an essential detail in our conversation) that pastoring by itself (without the devil), its current design, and its dynamics are positioned toward burnout.

Based on how pastoring has evolved, and the demands placed on modern pastors, pastoring is already positioned towards burnout, even without the devil. Most pastors do not realize (or are not even told) that when they start the journey, by design of the pastoring construct, they are already facing the slippery slope of burnout. The enemy is leveraging burnout as a tool. Be aware that the enemy is not technically creating all the nuances that create a burnout scenario.

> ***Knowledge Point:*** Based on how pastoring has evolved, pastoring is already positioned towards burnout, even without the devil.

The knowledge point notes that because of the evolution or changes to pastoring, individuals, even at the start of their pastoring journey, are already staring eye to eye with burnout. Let us look at the game Jenga ® as a reference point. The game starts with a tower of blocks with no gaps. Each player must remove a piece when it is their turn, which makes the tower unstable until eventually it falls. Pastoring is like this tower, except pastors start with a tower with blocks missing. It does not matter if a pastor is starting a church or coming into leadership in an established church; blocks will be missing.

This book and the solutions provided aim to help pastors stabilize their ministry and replace some of the missing blocks. This book will not address every missing block; however, we can help replace the ones related to burnout, as will be discussed. Every church is different, and each pastor will focus on different concerns; nonetheless, the goal is to build a strong, functioning church that represents Christ and allows individuals to grow, learn, and become more like Him. Conjoined to this thought is that research shows that many pastors have high job satisfaction when it comes to pastoring, meaning that at its core, they enjoy it. High job satisfaction does not diminish the energy, strength, spiritual discipline, and mental fortitude needed to lead a congregation. Pastoring and leading a church are not simple, regardless of how much a person enjoys it.

In a conversation about the secondary traumatization experience of pastors, the writers state without hesitation that life as a pastor can be a "hazardous journey."[7] The vocational demands can stress or frustrate the individual to the degree that they burn out.[8] Ironically, calling can be a motivational factor for some burned-out people.[9]

This is an important point about motivation, though it may seem counterintuitive. Since pastors view their calling as being from God, even if burned out, they will still

"...the clergy life can be a "hazardous journey."

push because they do not want to disappoint the one who called them. That is a difficult place to be as a pastor. To want to stop, take a break, throw in the towel, or leave your church – but because of who called you, even with no gas in the tank, pastors try to keep going. I do not think it was God's design for pastors to find themselves in this constant crucible, fighting burnout and trying to follow their calling; if so, this setup would seem cruel and unnecessary. There will be hard times and difficult moments, but pastors constantly battling burnout sound more like activity from an enemy than God.

Each of the nine pastors on this journey with us shares how following a call can affect a person's health and how drastic changes are often needed to preserve their well-being.

*(The following conversations and comments are from my research and dissertation on pastoral burnout).*[10]

Each of our pastors shared that ministry has the potential to impact their health. How a pastor interprets their calling can affect their life and overall health. Six out of nine pastors noted health concerns. Those who did experience health issues spoke about stress, increased blood pressure, unknown health issues, and health concerns exacerbated by the demands of the ministry. Reducing stressors can still be challenging even when pastors are mindful of their health. Pastor Daniel shared about the conflict between personal health and ministry.

**Pastor Daniel:**

> The conflict between my personal health and ministry was every day. I have had to quit a job because my blood pressure was extremely high. There was so much going on in the church that I had to let something go. My cardiologist was in shock when I was doing my yearly stress test because my blood pressure was so high. I was on the treadmill, and my cardiologist said, turn the machine off, turn the machine off! He quickly gave me a chair and asked how do you feel? I said I feel fine. I can run for miles. He said your blood pressure is currently so high; you should have had

a stroke at this moment. That is when reality hit me: You can follow your calling and do ministry work, but your health must come first.

Similarly, Pastor Julius spoke about health concerns stemming from pastoring and the need to monitor one's health.

**Pastor Julius:**

I have had several health-related situations that stem from my work as a pastor. The one thing I am grateful for is that I am at a stage and age where I have the grace to push through and make it through. However, I developed high blood pressure due to weight gain, which was due to an unknown underlying condition. Recently, my sleep patterns have been up and down, and my blood pressure rises when I do not have a good night's sleep. I also started having some issues with my lower back. So, yes, there are times when my health and calling collide. I am doing the best I can to push through. I am not doing ministry at the level I want to, but I am giving it my all, given my health.

Since stress as most people interpret it can be seen as a regular part of pastoring, individuals can easily ignore it when burnout and other issues arise as they try to advance in their calling. The dialogue about these pastors' experiences is not a negative thing. These are the experiences that these pastors and many other pastors have faced. Some pastors want to continue in ministry; however, their body has other plans. Pastor Esther agreed with Pastor Daniel about health issues, their connection to ministry, and their calling.

## Pastor Esther:

> The work of ministry started to catch up with me. I developed a heart condition, but I am glad the Lord protected me when I did not realize what was happening. I kept thinking it was asthma. I was short of breath at the time, and my first thought was asthma, not my heart. I was treating myself and using an inhaler. However, I was not getting better; I was getting worse. It got so bad that I could not carry stuff from downstairs without getting winded and wheezing. At that point, I mentioned it to my doctor, and after running some tests, my doctor referred me to a

cardiologist. I am seeing a cardiologist regularly and on medication. I am pretty sure church, combined with my job, is what contributed to my health issues.

The pastors who experienced health concerns expressed that the challenge is that the health issues form over time, and some go undetected. As pastors, they are doing the work of ministry, and their health is slowly suffering. However, the effects can take months, if not years, to appear. If individuals are not monitoring their health, they can encounter health issues later in ministry and life. Pastor Michael spoke about health concerns occurring over time.

## Pastor Michael:

When I was younger, I would drink large amounts of soda, and it took a toll on my body. I was unaware of doing it or that it would eventually have the effect I believe it had. I think a part of it may also be family genetics, but I do have a blood sugar condition that I have to monitor. I can become frustrated when I feel more tired on certain days because I see many things that could be done related to ministry that are positive and impactful. I do believe in physical healing. I believe Jesus can heal. Honestly, though, I do not dwell on my health too much. The people who love me think about my health often, but it is not something I am dwelling on.

The pastors noted that some things could be done to reduce health issues, such as changes in diet or more sleep. However, pastoring has stress and pressure that are not reduced easily. Pastor Nathan discussed how a doctor might suggest a preventive measure, although implementing it is not as simple when you have the responsibilities as a pastor.

## Pastor Nathan:

Health is a fact of life. I have had high blood pressure, and my doctor told me I need to reduce my stress, lower my sodium, and a few other things. As a pastor, it can be stressful. It is a stressful job because you see and experience a lot. One of my challenges is that I do not necessarily see the outcome of all my work immediately. So, you do not know if what you did or said was right, which can cause stress and mental fatigue. As a pastor, people trust you, and you want to give them the best information and direction you can, so when you are unsure or have to wait to see if you are right, that can burden you, but that is another story.

Similarly, Pastor Ryan acknowledged being aware and intentional about focusing on personal health to avoid burnout and other issues.

**Pastor Ryan:**

Naturally, the more you work, the more your body will feel the brunt of what you do. So, if you are not sleeping, exercising, or eating right, combined with the work of ministry and pastoring, that can be a recipe for disaster. If not addressed, all those activities will collide; the question is when the collision will happen. As a pastor, you feel the weight of ministry all the time. We have to make a conscious decision to take care of ourselves. I have been known for saying I refuse to let pastoring kill me. I believe it is a poor practice of discipline, and I do not follow what I see others doing related to poor health choices. I go and have my annual physical. If something is wrong, I schedule an appointment to see my doctor. I get at least six hours of sleep every night and exercise daily. When these areas are in conflict, and my health and body are not functioning right, I sit down and re-calibrate.

To take the conversation back to the initial thought, each pastor believed they were in their position because God called them there. Even though they have a call, complexities, such as health, force the pastors to make different decisions or even question their calling. The pastors shared that they were leading a church because they were called and felt they could achieve the desired outcome as a pastor with God's help. How the pastors interpret their calling in connection with their understanding of burnout will determine specific actions or non-actions related to ministry and addressing burnout.

Pastor Conner shared that *'calling'* is about the pastor's understanding that God is in control of the narrative. *"But many times, I believe as pastors, we get in the way of God, and we try to do it all and be it all."* The desire to keep going and not give up is not always external but an internal push.

As Pastor Daniel explained: *"When you are called, it just will not allow you to stop, or at least that is what it feels like."* Regardless of the person's feelings, they want to keep going because of their call. A Calling is not easy to compartmentalize, and each participant had to address calling through their lens and experience. Pastor Julius shared, *"I knew I was called to pastor. I knew God specifically wanted me to do it because of how everything transpired in my life. However, I did not want to accept pastoring. I avoided it for months."* Pastor Moses shared a personal experience with calling.

## Pastor Moses:

> Pastoring was not the path that I wanted to take. I was called into ministry when I was in my teens. However, I ignored the call and tried to live my life in such a way as to make myself unworthy of ministry, or so I thought. I did not accept my calling to ministry until I was in my 40's. Finally, accepting the call to pastor impacted my life significantly once I stopped running from God.

Even in accepting the call, the participants noted that there can still be internal conflicts due to wanting to pastor while knowing they did not *choose* to be called and could be doing something else with their lives. Pastor Ryan understood the call to ministry but was transparent in realizing his options. He stated, *"I could be doing a lot of other things with my time, but God has placed a strong conviction in my heart to where this is something I need to do."*

## Pastor Conner:

> I have been called to do this. Honestly, this was not the call I had in mind for my life. I did not want to be a pastor. I am clear about that with my church. I was okay working with youth at my other church, but God said, "I require more of you," in a clear voice. I decided it was best to listen to God. I decided long ago that whenever God tells me to do something, I will do it. So, here I am pastoring. I did not want to be here, and the truth be told, I do not want to be here now, but I am here. A call from God is a powerful thing.

Focusing on the fact that God is the one who called the participants is significant. The call to ministry was not from a friend or neighbor. It was a call from the God that they each believed in and served.

Pastor Michael simplified his thought by saying, *"I do not think about burnout. I know God has called me, so I show up."* Pastor Nathan furthered the conversation about serving God and following your call.

## Pastor Nathan:

I heard a call from the Lord, and I took that seriously. It is not about people, money, or anything else. It is not about having business acumen and knowing how to make a church financially successful. It is not about any of that. It is about whether I am faithful to the One who called me. I think that is important. In addition, am I doing it in a manner that is pleasing to Him? That way of thinking is what drives my actions. I am not worried about people's opinions or thoughts because they did not call me. I must answer to God. Period. This conviction of who called me is always at the back of my mind.

Similarly, Pastor Julius talked about being called and focusing on God.

**Pastor Julius:**

> When I think about the calling of God on my life to pastor and the doors that God has opened for me, it makes me adamant about making sure that I am doing what God wants. Whether I am tired or hurting, sore or discouraged, I could be sad on the inside, but I push that aside because of the calling on my life, and I find a way to compartmentalize my concerns. So, I can preach, teach, and pastor authentically in a manner that is pleasing to God.

Calling can also be why some pastors keep going and do not stop or give up. Following a calling and leading a church can be difficult and create moments of personal tension. Pastor Daniel noted that following a calling can bring a moment of wanting to give up, but the calling keeps pushing one to go forward.

## Pastor Daniel:

When you want to stop, the calling will not let you. When you have every reason on the left-hand side of the page why you should quit, and there is only one reason on the right side, and you stay because of that one thing, that is the power of a calling. That is the reality of it. You say, "I do not want to do this anymore." That moment only lasts for a few minutes, but it is a real moment and often intense. It is challenging because you honestly want to walk away. You try to give it up, but walking away when God calls is tough. These moments also remind you that He is with you.

The calling for the family or the spouse is not always the same as the pastor. However, the family is affected by the pastor's call

The married participants of this study explained that their spouse and family are intertwined in their calling. Pastor Moses shared, "Several individuals who are married to pastors said to my spouse that when God called me, they called my spouse as well." I do not doubt this to be true for the pastors who share this sentiment. It is important to note that the calling for the family or the spouse is not always the same as the pastor. However, the family is affected by the pastor's call. As Pastor Ryan shared, "The calling impacts those around me."

**Pastor Ryan:**

> The calling impacts those around me. Before we got married, I explained to my wife that I knew I was called to preach, but this calling was more extensive than I understood. So we have to be flexible. We have to be agile. We have to be ready for whatever God tells us to do so that we can stay together. We sometimes clash. However, my family is my number one ministry, and it starts with me pastoring my home before I pastor people.

Pastors follow a calling that compels them to continue pastoring and motivates them in their ministry. However, the calling does not reduce the environmental stressors that clergy face as they lead their church.

As we close out this chapter, pastors must be mindful of their call and how that call from God affects all areas of their lives. I am not telling you anything you do not already know as a pastor. This initial dialogue serves as our foundation, so we all work from the same body of knowledge. The call to lead a church is not easy. We can see that from all the individuals called to lead in the Bible. As we continue our conversation and hear from our pastors again in later chapters, we must remember that one of the motivations for continuing to go even when a pastor feels burned out is because they feel called. Calling is also why if a pastor leaves ministry due to burnout or other issues, they can harbor bitterness and anger toward God. How can God call me, leave me out there, let me become overwhelmed, or put me in such a negative situation? Burnout can blur or distort a pastor's view of God. Again, pastoring is not simple and not easy. The enemy is keen on finding ways to use burnout to push pastors to a place where they cannot do the work of ministry effectively, that they walk away from pastoring, or, in some cases, by ignoring their health, can suffer life-ending ordeals.

# Chapter Reflections:

1. What have been your experiences with burnout?

2. Has your calling and your health ever conflicted? If so, what did you do?

3. Do you feel as if you can relate to any of the pastors? If so, which one and why?

4. What additional thoughts or questions do you wish were covered in this chapter?

---


1. Dik, B. J., & Duffy, R. D. (2009). Calling and vocation at work: Definitions and prospects for research and practice. The Counseling Psychologist, 37(3), 424–450. https://doi.org/10.1177/0011000008316430

2. Christopherson, R. W. (1994). Calling and career in Christian ministry. Review of Religious Research, 35(3), 219–237. https://doi.org/10.2307/3511890

3. McKenna, R. B., Matson, J., Haney, D. M., Becker, O., Hickory, M. J., Ecker, D. L., & Boyd, T. N. (2015). Calling, the caller, and being called: A qualitative study of transcendent calling. Journal of Psychology and Christianity, 34(4), 294–303.

4. Duffy, R. D., Dik, B. J., Douglass, R. P., England, J. W., & Velez, B. L. (2018). Work as a calling: A theoretical model. Journal of Counseling Psychology, 65(4), 423–439. https://doi.org/10.1037/cou0000276

5. Conway, N., Clinton, M., Sturges, J., & Budjanovcanin, A. (2015). Using self-determination theory to understand the relationship between calling enactment and daily well-being. Journal of Organizational Behavior, 36(8), 1114–1131. https://doi.org/10.1002/job.2014

6. Dunbar, S., Frederick, T., Thai, Y., & Gill, J. (2020). Calling, caring, and connecting: burnout in Christian ministry. Mental Health, Religion & Culture, 23(2), 173–186. https://doi.org/10.1080/13674676.2020.1744548

7. Hendron, J. A., Irving, P., & Taylor, B. (2011). The unseen cost: A discussion of the secondary traumatization experience of the clergy. Pastoral Psychology, 61(2), 221–231. https://doi.org/10.1007/s11089-011-0378-z

8. Hendron, J. A., Irving, P., & Taylor, B. (2011). The unseen cost: A discussion of the secondary traumatization experience of the clergy. Pastoral Psychology, 61(2), 221–231. https://doi.org/10.1007/s11089-011-0378-z

9. Barnard, L. K., & Curry, J. F. (2012). The relationship of clergy burnout to self-compassion and other personality dimensions. Pastoral Psychology, 61(2), 149–163. https://doi.org/10.1007/s11089-011-0377-0

10. Washington, B. (2021). Understanding Burnout in Non-denominational Clergy: A Social Cognitive Approach (Doctoral dissertation, University of Southern California).

"Burnout, like any difficult experience, is a great teacher. My question is: What is it trying to tell you?"

— Dr. Rebecca Ray

# 3

# UNDERSTANDING BURNOUT

A problem-solving framework has two key components: understanding the problem and the context. Let us focus on understanding the problem first. That may sound simple, but we often treat symptoms rather than the problem.

> ***Burnout:*** a psychological syndrome of emotional exhaustion, depersonalization, and reduced personal accomplishment that can occur among individuals who work with other people in some capacity.[1]

If a person suffers from lower back pain, and we only look to treat the pain and not what is causing the pain, the person may continue through life using pain medicine because the source of the problem has not been determined. In this same scenario, a *good* doctor will first ask questions when a person seeks medical attention. The doctor is trying to assess how the person arrived at their current condition, understanding the problem and context.

Based on the answers to the questions and other tests, the doctor will prescribe a plan of treatment that hopefully addresses the source of the problem based on the context and the symptoms. Context in this scenario also includes the person's age, general health, underlying conditions, and background. This information (context) provides the canvas for the doctor to determine the issue and the proper treatment. The treatment for a 30-year-old athlete with lower back pain may be different from a non-active 78-year-old with underlying health conditions and lower back pain.

The solutions to most problems are often hidden. If a person is burned out, they will feel exhausted. The prescribed remedy is time away or rest, which is helpful, except it will not erase burnout. To address burnout in a comprehensive and long-term approach, a pastor will need more than a long weekend or a few extra naps on the sofa. The Bible instructs us, "In all thy getting, get understanding." (Proverbs 4:7)

For the sake of conversation, let us draw a parallel to our ability to share our faith. A Christian should be able to explain, expound, and express the critical components of Christianity

> "...the solutions to most problems are usually hidden."

and do the same regarding scripture and doctrine. That is to say, they should do more than quote scriptures or recite cliches. The average Christian may not be able to break down Greek and Hebrew; however, they should be able to easily explain the central tenets of our faith and provide context for any general questions that may arise from a non-Christian. The same understanding and approach should be utilized with burnout. I do not intend to give you all the nuances of burnout. However, as a pastor, you should know how burnout operates and the mechanisms that may trigger it in ministry.

***Knowledge Point***: Burnout happens over time.

Burnout does not happen in a day. If you have a sudden rush of fatigue or a reduced feeling of accomplishment, chances are that it is not burnout. Other conditions mirror burnout. The only difference is the trigger. For context, we will begin with burnout and then briefly look at similar conditions.

## The Slow Burn

Due to the expansion of online streaming services, many people will binge-watch a show's entire season. Whether it is a TV drama, a game show, or a cooking documentary, a person can curl up on their couch, get their favorite snacks, and spend all Saturday watching that show. If you grew up before the streaming era, then you know this was not how it was historically. If you had a show that aired every Tuesday or Wednesday, you had to be in front of the television at that specific time (unless you were fortunate enough to have a VCR).

Burnout does not happen in a day.

If you missed the show, there was not much you could do. You would have to rely on a secondhand account from somebody who watched the show to find out what happened. Burnout, in a singular sense, is very much like a season of a television show. It is a series of events, actions, decisions, and situations that crescendo to this grand finale that we identify as burnout. However, a person does not "binge burn out." Nobody burns out in one or two days, but as the season of our life unfolds, many people, especially pastors, find themselves heading toward burnout.

C.S. Lewis highlights the Law of Undulation in his classic book *The Screwtape Letters*. Life is full of ups and downs, and the enemy will attempt to use the ups and downs to challenge our faith or derail what God is doing in our lives. Burnout may not always be intense. Once a pastor has entered the place of burnout, it does not matter if they are on the mountain or in the valley; burnout is the song that is constantly playing. Sometimes, the music is loud; sometimes, there is barely a whisper, but burnout is still there. *Note:* Great experiences and euphoric moments do not erase burnout. That song (burnout) will continue to play unless a pastor intentionally goes through steps to "turn off" burnout.

Unlike the shows we watch where the drama and tension are created and constructed, thus not genuine, the pain, hurt, and frustration of a pastor facing burnout is accurate, and there

> Great experiences and euphoric moments do not erase burnout.

is often no way for them to say, "Cut!" The reality we all live in does not stop, even for those burning out. Please note the following: _time will not rid you of burnout._ A person cannot outgrow or outrun burnout. To find a remedy for burnout, a pastor must be intentional. It will not happen by accident.

## More Than a Myth

Joseph Fichter wrote a historical paper entitled "The Myth of Clergy Burnout." In the article, he attempted to promote the concept that pastors should not burn out. Fichter's rationale was that since pastors are connected to God, there was no possible way for them to burn out.[2] I can tell you definitively that he was wrong, well, sort of. He said if you prayed and did all God had for you to do, you would be able to stand and not give into the "weakness" of burnout. Fichter may have been onto something in the statements related to "doing what God called pastors to do." Suggesting that if a pastor oversteps that boundary, they will be suspectable to burnout.

> "...time will not rid you of burnout. A person cannot outgrow or outrun burnout."

That could be true; however, our current research would suggest otherwise, as we will discuss shortly. Burnout is real, and if you are facing burnout, you are not weak or any other label that people put on individuals who face the reality of being burned out. A study of 1,050 pastors found that "100% of the pastors surveyed knew of a fellow pastor who had experienced compassion fatigue or burnout, with 90% stating that they felt fatigued or worn out on a weekly or daily basis."[3] This study was pre-COVID, and we know that pastors experienced a higher level of burnout during parts of 2019 through 2022 due to the COVID-19 pandemic.

As you read this, do you know of a pastor who is burned out, or are you that pastor who feels the daily effects of burnout? In the 2021 article in the *Journal of Pastoral Theology* entitled, "Distinguishing Between the Pastor and the Superhero: God on Burnout and Self-Care," the researcher expressed that burnout could not be a myth for those who lead God's people.[4] The writer pointed to the Biblical example of Moses. God instructed Moses to lead the children of Israel. His entire ministry was focused on leading millions of Israelites from Egypt to the Promised Land. During that time, Moses experienced burnout, costing him his ministry.

In Numbers Chapter 20, Moses, in frustration, strikes the rock to draw water from it instead of speaking to it as God instructed him. God told Moses he would not lead the people into the land He promised them because of Moses' disobedience. Remember our initial conversation, which started in Chapter 1? Burnout is subtle. If left unchecked, it will ruin our life, ministry, and relationship with God. Burnout is the optimal tool for carrying out the devil's plan to "steal, kill and destroy," according to John 10:10. Working with people can be difficult, and people who work primarily with people tend to face burnout at a higher rate.

Ask any teacher trying to instruct students who would rather talk and not pay attention. Ask any person who works in customer service, and they will tell you that working with people is not easy. People are not reasonable; they are self-centered and selfish. In the book *The Prince,* the writer expresses that all leaders should know that people are habitually ungrateful and fickle. Read that again: unless the power of God has changed a person, their default setting is to be ungrateful, fickle, and self-serving. Working with people is complex, and working with people in the church community can be more difficult.

## Pastors vs. Other Helping Professionals

Earlier in the chapter, we discussed understanding the problem and context. To provide more context, pastors seem to reside in an arena alone. However, this is not an accurate depiction. Pastors are helping professionals. Helping professionals are people who predominantly collaborate (or work) with people.[5] Teachers, social workers, police officers, physicians, and nurses are all helping professionals. Following the COVID-19 pandemic, much of the research (and rightfully so) focused on healthcare professionals; even before the COVID-19 pandemic, pastors were left out of studies related to helping professionals. The reason is that the role of a pastor is not straightforward compared to a surgeon or police officer.

The pastor's role is dynamic, unstable, and sometimes even perilous. Pastoring can be unpredictable. As a pastor, think about the most unpredictable thing that has happened in your church. Even now, you look back, scratch your head, and wonder, "What were they thinking," or "Why did I allow them to do that?" People post on social media now and laugh about conflicts in church. However, there is nothing funny about those situations. The pastor will have to navigate through the aftermath and figure out how to mend or put back in order something that they were not expecting to happen. Not to digress, but a lot happens in church, much of which is outside of the pastor's control, and we should add to every pastor's resume the job of a referee.

Being a pastor is "hard work," contrary to popular belief. I have witnessed people dismiss the work somebody has done at a church and think that church work is not real work. Getting people from different walks of life to focus on Jesus, increase their faith, and to be built up in unity and love is not a simple task. People forget that people who come to church, whom pastors have to lead (I am preaching to the choir), are essentially volunteers. If a person is not on the payroll at the church, there is not much a pastor can do to get them to do more as a volunteer. The pastor (and the church leaders) must be masterful in presenting truth from scripture as directed by the Holy Spirit, which elicits conviction and contemplation without pushing congregants into offense so that they harden their hearts and walk away from the Truth.

Every Sunday, a pastor must be a surgeon rightly dividing the Word of Truth, pondering whether they did well, and ensuring not to injure while using the scripture to "divide between soul and spirit." The work may look simple to those outside the church, but pastoring is more than Sunday morning, as we will unpack in the following chapters.

Unlike other helping professionals, pastors are on call 24/7, even with boundaries. People say, "set boundaries." Do this and turn off that. For most pastors, that is a difficult task, and it is not easy to "turn off or tune out" the people you must lead. Pastors have to balance preserving the well-being of parishioners and their well-being. Research shows that pastors spend about 20% of the workweek in counseling sessions. Pastors are viewed as on-demand assistance.[6] For most therapists or doctors, individuals make appointments and cannot directly contact the doctor at will. In churches, however, this is not always the case. Depending on the church's size or location, members could have direct access to the pastor.[7] [8]

In the article "Maintaining Personal Resiliency: Lessons Learned from Evangelical Protestant Clergy," the researchers noted that pastors have become "therapists on demand."[9]Think about what that statement says about pastors, both directly and implied. People think pastors should be available when they need them, and they should be able to help with whatever concerns they have. Those are weighty expectations to place on somebody.

To continue this conversation, let us quickly compare pastors to physicians to understand why Pastors are more susceptible to burnout. For this conversation, as defined by the American Medical Association (AMA), a physician is any medical person with a Doctor of Medicine degree (MD) or equivalent. Let us examine roles, family, working hours, and code of conduct concerning pastors and physicians. The following paragraphs are for additional context so that individuals can better see how pastors differ from other helping professionals.

## Roles (Subtopic)

Physicians have defined roles, and their roles have minimal deviation. For example, a surgeon will not be an ambulance driver. The doctor in the Emergency Room will not do the intake paperwork for a patient in a car accident. The physician's role is strictly defined, and it could even be a violation or issue if they decide to do something outside of what they are qualified to do. Now, pastors are different. The role of the pastor is not singular and constantly changes. *Social Work and Christianity* researchers stated that pastors must address "unrealistic, ambiguous demands and boundary intrusion from congregants."[10] Consider if this statement rings true based on your pastoral journey.

Pastors are leaders, friends, therapists, presenters of religious thoughts, community leaders, church van drivers, Sunday school teachers, and so on. Depending on the size of the church

> pastors must address "unrealistic", ambiguous demands and boundary intrusion from congregants

and support (staff), a pastor will move between roles multiple times daily and must do it seamlessly.

## Family (subtopic)

In the article "Demand, Support, and Perception in Family-Related Stress Amongst Protestant Clergy," the writers stated that a pastor's family would incur undue stress.[11] The stress on the family is not new, but let us expound on it. The congregation's expectation of the pastor is almost always levied on the family. *The Journal of Religion and Health* details this in the article "The Relationship Between Work-related Stress and Boundary-related Stress within the Clerical Profession." The pastor's family is expected to operate similarly to the pastor, and the pastor's work often restricts and encroaches on the family's time and space, as noted. The pastor's work often breaches the established boundaries, can be unpredictable, and consumes half of the weekend due to Sunday obligations. One of the leading complaints spouses raise is the amount of time consumed by the ministry, as highlighted in the article "Denominational Support for Clergy Mental Health" from the *Journal of Psychology and Theology*.

Researchers point out that the pastor's family is assumed to be perfect and is always displayed as the epitome of how a family should act and interact. Some of these norms have changed;

however, plenty of expectations are placed on the pastor's family that other helping professionals do not have to address. A physician's family is not judged by the same metrics as the physician. Yes, I acknowledge we are talking about a spiritual role with a call by God. This component, however, makes pastoring more complex and opens the door for burnout. I would argue that no one has left a top physician because of the disposition of the physician's spouse.

Nobody has ever inquired why a physician's spouse does not work in their private practice. Most people probably do not care what a physician's family does, provided the physician does their job well. Imagine if the church treated pastors the same. For example, the pastor's entire family did not have to be tied into the church; the pastor's spouse did not automatically have to lead specific ministries or be at every event. That is not to say that their family does not want to be in church; however, people forget that the pastor's family also wants to come to church without being under the microscope of the parishioners.

## Working Hours (subtopic)

Physicians and pastors often work long hours. Depending on what area a physician focuses on determines their work schedule and how busy they will be each day. Even though physicians can have long hours when they finish work, they are actually off work. When they leave the office, they are not expected back until their next work day. Pastors are in demand 24/7. At a larger church, perhaps not as much, but the demands and responsibilities are different. I visited a mega church in the US years ago, and I was surprised to see all the extra auxiliaries that the ministry needed for a Sunday service.

They had police directing traffic, two ambulances out front of the church, security, and people directing you where to park, and all this was happening outside the building. The pastor does not monitor those activities personally, though they are needed because of the size of the church. In addition, the pastor's work schedule is not always predictable, whether the church is large or smaller. Pastors can receive calls at any hour of the night. Even with boundaries, pastors receive calls, texts, and emails updating them, informing them, or letting them know that something happened related to the church.

## Code of Conduct

Physicians must abide by the Hippocratic Oath and the Health Insurance Portability and Accountability Act (HIPAA) laws. These nearly universally held philosophies and laws provide practitioners and patients with a degree of comfort and compliance. When patients fail to comply, they suffer a lack of care. Pastors have a code of conduct; it is the Bible. However, we all have been privy to how different pastors have handled certain situations. Let me repeat this, and let us all be honest: since we have different Christian reformations, the Bible is the code of conduct. However, each reformation will interpret it differently. These differences can be seen in the example of "dual relationships."

One researcher stated, "Clergy, unlike other helping professionals, do not adhere to a standard code of ethics that provides or sets guidelines and rules for dual relationships. Dual relationships are instances wherein a helping professional and a client [congregant] share multiple roles."[12] For example, a pastor could be counseling an individual who is going through a divorce, serve under that person on the school board, and that person could be an old high school friend. There is no set structure or general guidelines for managing these complex relationships.

Pastors often lead their families, instruct their siblings, counsel their friends, and journey with relatives through the intricacies of life. There is no set way to handle these interactions save for the leading of the Holy Spirit. Pastors are often in situations that have no direct instruction or code of conduct to guide them. As a side note, there may be rules within denominations, but those rules do not always cover these relationship dynamics as outlined. Also, the rise of more independent and non-denominational churches with internal governing structures, varying approaches to administration, and minimal external oversight creates additional complexities for pastors.

## Movability

I have a good friend who is a police officer. Police officers are also helping professionals. I also know another individual who is a doctor. The doctor formerly worked in the emergency room for a large hospital. Both individuals realized that the environment at their respective jobs was not benefiting them. So, they dusted off their resumes, applied to other jobs, and moved on. A doctor facing burnout at a clinic can find a new job and remain a doctor. A police officer or teacher can apply to another city or educational district. For this conversation, we will define movability as a person's ability to move within their profession or area of expertise without hindrance or penalty.

For pastors, the idea of movability is almost non-existent. First, let us look at movability within denominations. A pastor within a denomination can want to leave a church for various reasons; however, there has to be another church to move them to, and the bishop or whoever oversees them must agree with the transition. In denominations, most people are looking to pastor the already established churches; the smaller churches that need more help are not ideal for most people. So, a pastor can be burned out, and if they leave their church, they are not guaranteed the ability to keep pastoring, though they have more chances to move to a new church within a denomination.

Before we move on, I intentionally explained the process of moving within a denomination in a simplified form. Many other factors and layers can be involved in a pastor's move to another church within a denomination. That being said, moving within a denomination is possible but not always optimal, depending on the situation. For example, a pastor in a denomination may want to move from their current church in Pittsburgh, PA, yet the only viable church that would fit what they are looking for is in Pensacola, FL. The move is available but not always optimal, depending on the individual and their situation.

Now, independent and non-denominational pastors are very unlikely to be able to move. If a pastor started a church, where can they go? If a pastor inherited the church, where can they go? So again, unlike other helping professionals, pastors often have to stay where they are because the option to move is unavailable. Also, moving or " abandoning" a church can create other issues and concerns. Again, we are simplifying the conversation because the focus is on the movement restrictions that pastors often face. For the non-denominational or independent pastor, it does not mean they cannot move to another church. Some churches have vacancies and advertise for pastoral roles. Perhaps the current pastor at the church left or had a medical condition, family situation, or some other circumstance that created a vacancy there.

Vacancies happen, but the options are usually few; just because options are available does not mean they will fit the pastor. For example, style of worship, belief, doctrine, structure, salary, and location all play into the movability conversation. Other helping professionals have more options within their immediate proximity; the work, expectations, and rules are usually very similar, and there is minimal backlash for those professionals when they move to a new job. Sometimes, those people are celebrated when they move on, especially if they find a better opportunity. A pastor leaving a church for greener pastures or due to burnout can cause quite a disturbance. In an October 2023 article, a pastor outlined why they were leaving their church, and the article noted that a high percentage of pastors (more than 40%) have considered quitting being a pastor.

The article touches on some areas related to burnout covered in this book; however, my attention was drawn to the comments on the article. The comments were a mix of understanding from those who have experienced burnout to those judging, casting blame and doubt on this pastor. A pastor exiting the ministry due to burnout is never a leisurely departure for the individual or the congregation.

Compared to other helping professionals, pastors are faced with an ambiguous terrain. Pastors have multiple roles, pressure on their families, irregular work schedules, no code of conduct, and the inability to move; these all point to burning out. I am not saying this because I do not think pastors are unaware.

I am confirming what you may have already thought about and know: pastoring is more than just a sermon on Sunday, and too many people (inside and outside the church) do not realize it. In the next chapter, you will hear from the nine pastors we met and heard from earlier. They will provide insight into burnout and their experiences, and we will start to bring things together and answer the questions that most pastors have related to burnout.

# Chapter Reflections:

1. As a pastor, have you thought about how many roles you occupy?

2. What is one role that you currently have that you wish you could pass on to somebody else?

3. How would you describe your congregation's understanding of your roles, and do you believe they understand everything you (and your family) do to keep the church functioning?

4. What is one thing that stuck out to you from this chapter (or the previous chapter) that you never considered related to your pastoral duties?

---


1.  Schaufeli, W. B., & Maslach, C. (1993). Professional burnout (1st ed.). Routledge. https://doi.org/10.4324/9781315227979

2. Fichter, J. H. (1984). The myth of clergy burnout. Sociological Analysis, 45(4), 373–382. https://doi.org/10.2307/3711300

3. Krejcir, R. J. (2007). Statistics on pastors: What is going on with the pastors in America? Francis A. Schaeffer Institute of Church Leadership Development. http://pirministries.org/wp-content/uploads/20 16/01/FASICLD-Statistics-on-Pastors.pdf

4. Samushonga, H.M. (2021). Distinguishing between the pastor and the superhero: God on burnout and self-care. Journal of Pastoral Theology, 31(1), 4–19. https://doi.org/10.1080/10649867.2020.1748919

5. Schaufeli, W. B., & Maslach, C. (1993). Professional burnout (1st ed.). Routledge. https://doi.org/10.4324/9781315227979

6. Jacobson, J. M., Rothschild, A., Mirza, F., & Shapiro, M. (2013). Risk for burnout and compassion fatigue and potential for compassion satisfaction among clergy: Implications for social work and religious organizations. Haworth Press.

7.  Barnard, L. K., & Curry, J. F. (2012). The relationship of clergy burnout to self-compassion and other personality dimensions. Pastoral Psychology, 61(2), 149–163. https://doi.org/10.1007/s11089-011-0377 -0

8. Parker, P. D., & Martin, A. J. (2011). Clergy motivation and occupational well-being: Exploring a quadripolar model and its role in predicting burnout and engagement. Journal of Religion and Health, 50(3), 656–674. https://doi.org/10.1007/s10943-009-9303-5

9. In the article "Maintaining Personal Resiliency: Lessons Learned from Evangelical Protestant Clergy," the researchers noted that pastors have become "therapists on demand."

10. Bledsoe, T. S., Setterlund, K., Adams, C. J., Fok-Trela, A., & Connolly, M. (2013). Addressing pastoral knowledge and attitudes about clergy/mental health practitioner collaboration. Social Work & Christianity, 40(1), 23–45.

11. Lee, C., & Iverson-Gilbert, J. (2003). Demand, support, and perception in family-related stress among protestant clergy. Family Relations, 52(3), 249–257. https://doi.org/10.1111/j.1741-3729.2003.00249.x

12. Wells, C. R., Probst, J., Mckeown, R., Mitchem, S., & Whiejong, H. (2012). The relationship between work-related stress and boundary-related stress within the clerical profession. Journal of Religion and Health, 51(1), 215–230. https://doi.org/10.1007/s10943-011-9501-9

"Suspecting and knowing
are not the same."

— Rick Riordan

# 4

# Pastor's Personal Thoughts on Burnout

The importance of knowing what we are looking for cannot be understated. If we misdiagnose, place too much emphasis in the wrong place, or misunderstand the symptoms of burnout, then a person can be heading into dangerous territory and be unaware.

***Knowledge Point:*** The correct definition and understanding of burnout are essential to addressing it.

If you have a vehicle and the oil should be changed every 3,000 miles, you should change the oil when you reach that mark. If you do not go by the mileage but wait until the oil light comes on, you may be at a point of damaging your engine, and the oil should be changed immediately. If you think the oil should not be changed until the engine is smoking, then the engine is already damaged and probably will need repairs. We should all note that knowing *what* and *when* is vital for our spiritual maintenance. Let me say that again: knowing *what* and *when* is imperative to our spiritual maintenance. Again, consider your car. In your car, there are many fluids that the car needs in order to run correctly. However, you do not handle each of those fluids in the same way. You need gas more frequently than you need to change your oil, and you may need more or less windshield wiper fluid depending on the weather conditions.

So, it is essential to know what we are trying to address so we apply the appropriate framework and steps for remediation. Changing your oil and forgetting about the gas or not changing the oil but continuing to get gas will land a person in the same position: stuck on the side of the road with an inoperable vehicle. Too many leaders and pastors (not intentionally) are waiting until smoke is billowing out from under their clergy collar to realize that something is wrong. However, the oil light and other indicators have been blinking profusely, indicating something is wrong.

In my 2021 study, 56% of the pastors noted that they had experienced burnout on a personal level. The remaining 44% had not encountered burnout personally, though they had seen it in colleagues or while serving as an assistant pastor.[1] Pastor Daniel explained his experience with burnout, "I began to struggle with the things that normally come easy. It was like I was being pulled and had no control over anything around me." This feeling of being pulled is what was noted earlier. Burnout was now driving the car, and Pastor Daniel did not intentionally give the keys to burnout. However, burnout ended up in the driver's seat, controlling his personal and spiritual life.

For pastors who have been in this position, this can be an unsettling or frightening place. To know that something is wrong and not be sure how to address it, or trying to address it and nothing is changing. Once burnout starts controlling your life, you cannot simply hit the brakes, and everything will stop. It does not work in that manner. I have used the analogy of a car to parallel the life of a pastor, though a tractor-trailer may be a better example in this case. Think about a tractor-trailer (18-wheeler) careening down a hill with a full load. Hitting the brakes will not stop that vehicle. Similarly, as you attempt to address burnout, it may seem like you are going further down a road you do not want to be on.

When discussing burnout, our nine pastors understood burnout through four primary lenses: Overwhelmed, Productivity, Emptiness, and Despair. Most pastors will fall into one of these four categories when they experience burnout. These things are not burnout but the realization that something is wrong and the person needs to take a step back. Think of these feelings as the oil light coming on. It is time to find the nearest mechanic to see what is going on.

## Drinking From a Fire Hose (Overwhelmed)

The pastors who described burnout through the experience of being overwhelmed spoke about having too many responsibilities or roles. There was a feeling (or need) to fulfill ALL church-related obligations. This overabundance of demands exhausted them and led to burnout.

Pastor Michael expressed that in moments of burnout, *"it feels as if everybody is demanding something from you, and you realize that you cannot meet that demand because you are only one person."*

Pastor Jessica stated, *"Burnout is when a person does not balance their personal and professional life and, as a result, becomes overwhelmed."* Pastor Michael said, *"Burnout can fall into different categories. There is physical burnout. There is spiritual burnout, and then there is being overwhelmed, which can be a mixture of things."*

Remember, these are each of these pastors' experiences. These experiences align with what other pastors have said. Everyone wants the pastor's attention, yet the pastor is only one person. Two hundred members and one hundred of them have an issue, and they only want to speak with the pastor. The members' problems are often outside the church, yet the church must address them. Pastors usually assist members with problems that the church has little to no control over, yet the problems cannot be ignored. If the pastor does not at least listen to the problems, they will often incur "spillover." Spillover is when personal issues outside the church begin to affect the church's operations. Keeping church, work, and home from colliding is tricky, depending on the issue. Again, the pastor is the only person the members want to assist them.

# I Can Do It, But I am Not Doing It (Unproductive)

When a person is burning out, their cognitive ability is hindered. They have the capacity, but simple tasks become difficult because of what they are experiencing. When a person has too much happening, the part of the brain responsible for creativity or developing thoughts is hampered. When I was growing up, desktop computers would slow down, and you had to defragment (or defrag) the computer. Due to all the programs running, "fragments" must be erased or removed so the computer can operate smoothly. A pastor who is burned out will operate, but not at the God-given capacity that they were designed.

> When a person is burning out, their cognitive ability is hindered

Let me add a note here. Research shows that prayer, meditation, and worship can assist with clearing our thoughts. Those solutions, however, cannot be used to address burnout fully in most cases. These are short-term solutions because they do, in fact, clear the mind and build up our spirit, but if the pastor's environment is still chaotic, they will once again become unproductive. Relating to the computer example, if I restart the computer and then go back and open all the same programs and documents I had before the restart, the computer will once again slow down. How many pastors have gone on vacation and returned feeling refreshed, only to walk into the same situation they left, and within a couple of weeks, it is as if they never had the vacation?

Pastor Daniel shared, *"Instead of being ahead of deadlines, I barely met them."* Though having not experienced burnout personally but being close to people who have burned out, Pastor Nathan explained, *"I consider fatigue similar to dimming a light or a lamp. However, burnout is when a person is ineffective and continuing in that condition is not sustainable."* He continued, *"Burnout is when you reach the point of not functioning effectively in the key areas of your life. I compare it to the process of a candle burning out. The candle is no longer producing light. The candle is not dim; it is extinguished. The pastor who is facing burnout is in that same condition. They are leading their church, yet they are not producing light. That is burnout."*

Pastor Daniel added, *"Burnout is when you are frustrated because nothing is getting done, and you are the reason why it is not getting done. Burnout is when your creativity and spiritual connectivity are gone; you are up at the pulpit ready to preach but have nothing to say, and you have been studying all week."*

Some pastors are burned out and can continue to function, though the light is not as bright or radiant as it should be. Then there are the cases where pastors have reached a point of being unable to produce anything. The frustration, as Pastor Daniel explained, *"is that as a pastor, we know the issue is not with God; the issue is with us, and we are unable to do what God has called us to do."*

## Pastor Conner

*Burnout is the covering or the oppression of passion. The person's passion or desire is there, but so many things cover that passion that the light cannot reach the surface. When burnout occurs, a person knows they can do the tasks set before them, but they do not accomplish them.*

For every pastor reading this, there is help for this situation, and your passion and light will not continue to be covered.

## Nothing to Pour Out (Emptiness)

Pastor Moses spoke about his experience seeing other clergy burnout: *"Those guys just poured and poured and poured, and nothing was given back to them."* Pastor Julius spoke from a personal experience and noted the feeling of wanting to keep going. However, it felt like there was no fuel to keep going:

*"You are essentially trying to pour from an empty cup."* Pastor Moses said, *"Burnout is when someone has hit the wall. They have an empty tank and nothing left to give. The person has ignored or neglected self-care; they poured out to others but never replenished themselves."* Pastor Julius stated, *"Burnout is being tired and empty. The person has run out of the strength to do what is necessary."* Pastor Julius' statement raises the point of self-care, which is essential but does not cure burnout. Every week, a pastor pours out, and if they cannot replenish themselves or the light has become so dim that they cannot gain strength, they will eventually start to pour from an empty cup.

## What Should I Do (Despair)

Finally, the pastors touched on despair. If despair or these other areas go unaddressed, they will lead to more severe problems. These pastors noted from their personal experience and seeing other pastors that you reach a point where you (want to) give up. Everything has gotten so unmanageable that you cannot do it anymore. When an individual reaches this point of despair, they cannot see how they will get through things and feel that nothing they do matters or changes things.

Pastor Esther shared a time when so much was happening personally and with the church, *"it just seemed like all my help was crumbling around me."*

Pastor Ryan stated, *"Burnout is when you say I cannot take this. I am tapped out; there is nothing left."*

These pastors described their experience with burnout, what they perceived it as, or how to explain it. As a pastor, have you experienced any of these scenarios? Or have you seen a colleague in a position like the one described? The results of burnout can be displayed in many different ways; however, we must remember the definition of burnout and its root cause. Knowing the definition of burnout is similar to your car notifying you of your upcoming oil change. If we ignore the notification and ride until smoke or fire is coming from the engine, we are past the point of burnout. At this point, we are on our way to damaging our life or even losing it.

# Case Study Considerations:

1. Can you, as a pastor, empathize or relate to the experiences of these pastors?

2. Have you personally or have you observed a colleague dealing with the effects of burnout?

---

1. Washington, B. (2021). Understanding Burnout in Non-denominational Clergy: A Social Cognitive Approach (Doctoral dissertation, University of Southern California).

"A wrong sum can be put
right: but only by going
back till you find the error
and working it afresh
from that point, never by
simply going on."

— C.S. Lewis,
The Great Divorce

# 5

# SELF-CARE IS NOT THE FINAL ANSWER

When my wife and I were preparing for our oldest daughter's birth, we were transitioning. We moved from an apartment to a condo, and things went well. We had finished setting up the nursery in our new place. My wife had done a fantastic job. It had this beautiful soft lavender paint on the wall, fresh carpet on the floor, matching lamps, baby blankets, and a pristine white changing table. The room had large floor-to-ceiling windows, and the sun's rays would enter and dance on the butterfly décor. The room felt warm and inviting. As my wife was sitting on the floor putting together a small piece of furniture, she saw something, and her heart sank. She did not want to get too close, so she called me and told me to look under the windowsill, and when I saw it, I knew we had a problem. There was mold. After calling a company to confirm that it was indeed mold, we were informed that it was not only under the windowsill but also inside the exterior wall. Long story short, we had to seal off a part of the condo and have the mold remediated. We had issues with the contractor, the condo association, and other delays. It took about nine months before the nursery and condo were back together and fit for use.

I am sharing that story because burnout is like the mold we found in our daughter's nursery. The mold had been there when we moved in. It was in the air. However, we were not in that room often, so it did not affect us; plus, most of it was hidden within the exterior wall. We were on the top floor, and there was an issue with the roof and the siding. Due to poor construction, water had gotten behind the wall, and mold began to fester. Burnout, as we said before, happens over time. It is a series of events that cause burnout. No singular event causes burnout. The difficulty of addressing burnout in pastors is that the solutions often provided to pastors are imbalanced and do not consider the broader scope of what is causing the burnout. The narrowness of the solutions available to pastors is why self-care can help, but it is not the final answer. We are not throwing away self-care. We are redefining its place in the solutions for burnout.

Burnout is like mold.  If left untreated, it will cause a significant problem. You do not address mold by simply leaving the mold-infested place. Yes, you will reduce mold's effect on you by not being co-located where it is, though you have not technically addressed the actual issue.

See the solutions of vacation, prayer, boundaries, friends, hobbies, and finding people to confide in place all the work on the pastor. What if the pastor is not to blame?  If we used the self-care model for the mold, we would stay in the place until the mold affected us, then we would leave the house, perhaps go someplace with fresh and clean air, and stay for a while. Once we no longer felt the effects of the mold, we would return to the house and stay until we felt the effects of the mold and then leave again. The issue is not with the person. The issue is with the environment. For some pastors, the issue is not with them. The issue is their church dynamics, congregation, denominational structure, or the constraints they face in their local assembly. Self-care (for some people) is leaving toxic to feel better, to return to toxic only to leave again when the symptoms return. In essence, the pastor who ascribes only to this version of the self-care model, save the Lord intervenes, is in a destructive cycle that can potentially harm them. Remember, just because you feel rested does not mean you have addressed burnout. Read that again slowly. Just because you feel rested does not mean you have addressed the issue of burnout.

Pastors have been directed to overlook the environmental factors, leaving the door open for a cycle of continued burnout.

> ***Knowledge Point***: Burnout is due to a combination of environmental and personal factors.

## Sabbaticals Revisited

Before we transition to exploring the pastoral environment, I want to caution us against thinking that self-care in the form of sabbaticals is the magic pill that solves burnout. Sabbaticals seem to have become the gold standard or best practices for pastors. Sabbaticals are not bad. However, they are exclusive and unavailable to every pastor, so it is not the optimal approach to burnout. Note that I am not saying that you should not take a sabbatical. Sabbaticals allow the pastor time to realign with God, think, pray and seek God concerning their personal life and the church. Sabbaticals, however, will not cure burnout, though they can assist in prolonging the life of a pastor. At the lowest common denominator being overworked is at the core of burnout.

Sabbaticals should not be seen as the remedy for burnout

So, if I go on sabbatical and return and the workload is the same, I will have more energy, though I will slowly start to burn out again. The main point here is that every pastor cannot take a sabbatical. With more than 70% of churches in the US having only one leader, it is hard to walk away for a sabbatical. The church also must agree to a sabbatical, and they have to agree to financial compensation as well. In addition, every pastor is not in full-time ministry, so if a pastor has a secular job and leads a church, it will be difficult to leave both obligations. Again, I am not against sabbaticals, though we may want to reconsider using them as the standard. Pastors should take time away to focus on God, reflect, pray, study, and reconnect with God. Sabbaticals should not be seen as the remedy for burnout. They should be seen as a time to commune with God.

In academics, when we revisit something, it means that we have arrived at another vantage point or additional information is available, so we should look at our original conclusion and see if it still holds true in the face of the new information. I want us to look at Genesis and the creation story. The creation story is where some people look related to a day of rest where God rested after he created the earth and Adam. The other point of reference is the Ten Commandments (Exodus 20:9-10) where God says that there are six days to work and to keep the Sabbath holy and to rest. Either way let us look at this idea of rest with a focus on Genesis.

> "By the seventh day, God had finished the work he had been doing; so on the seventh day, he rested from all his work.  Then God blessed the seventh day and made it holy because on it he rested from all the work of creating that he had done." – Genesis 2: 2-3 (NIV)

I want us to look at this scripture through a different lens. Let us not focus initially on the day of rest at the end. God is showing us something about our lives and ministry in the preceding six days.

The first is that God had a plan with an end goal. How do we know this? After he had formed a world conducive to man's living, he formed man and then stopped.  How many of us have a plan?

Second is that God did not overload his days. Remember, God has a plan, so each day has a specific objective. He did not try to separate night and day and form the birds of the air. When we read Genesis, we can quickly look at each day and know His intent, and when He finished that objective, He stopped.

Third, the plan had a specific sequence. God did not form the fish without first forming the water to put them in. He did not form man without having a place to put Him. God created a structure for the earth's development for humanity's benefit. God shows us through creation that *planning, process, and patience* are essential. Remember, He is God. Do we think God could not have formed all this in a day? When it comes to ministry, we need a plan, a process, and patience. The plan, process, and patience allow us to rest on the seventh day. I will say that again. A pastor is afforded rest when they have a plan, a process, and patience. We cannot pack our schedules, have multiple plans in operation, and then wonder why we cannot rest. The day (or time) to rest is a product of a structured plan.

Finally, God was singular in his focus. We can assume other things might have occurred, but once God starts forming the earth and ultimately creating man, he does not focus on anything else. He is not conversing with the angels or looking at other planets and solar systems. Based on what we see in scripture for these six days, God focused solely on creating the earth and his masterpiece, man. Most of our churches do a poor job of focusing on a singular endeavor. For example, a church needs a new roof. The main project is raising money to repair the roof. If the focus is to repair the roof, everything that stretches the budget or unnecessarily utilizes money should be avoided.

Stewardship prompts leaders to prioritize purpose and vision over ceremony. This is not an indictment but an observation of the many tough trade-offs church leaders face in preserving historical landmarks while plotting a course for new ones.

When looking at burnout, *planning,* and *patience* are keys to *preservation.* We cannot do everything all at once, and every church cannot provide every service or ministry, which is ok. A study by the Barna Group on leadership amongst Senior Pastors in Protestant churches found that 92% of those surveyed felt great at leading and motivating people. However, the issue is that only 14% of those same individuals felt good at *strategic leadership.* As Barna points out, most pastors are *directing leaders,* or *visionary leaders,* which is a style of leadership usually opposite of strategic leadership principles. I do not want us to overlook this. Doing too much, not having a plan, shooting from the hip, and saying I will do it because "God said it" are recipes for disasters. If we use the Bible as our guideline, when God told people to move in faith or do something, there were directions in almost every instance. *God is not looking for "super churches". He is looking for churches that are making an impact in the way he designed, under the leadership of pastors who have a heart for Him.*

**Knowledge Point:** Not having a plan or process when leading an organization will lead to burnout.

Plans are helpful because there are success points. So, as a leader, you can quantify your success. Please do not say results do not matter. They do. Nobody will continue to do anything, even follow God, without results. People went to the prophets in the Old Testament because of the results. So, having a plan can reduce the potential for burnout and increase our motivation. A pastor can then point to specific goals or successes, allowing the congregation to see progress.

Pastors will burn out without a definitive plan for their ministry. What has God said, what is He saying, and how do we align with that? There may be a gap in funding or other resources, but the plan allows the leader to see those areas and devise a strategy to tackle them. We all know that to reduce debt, a person needs a plan. The person must reduce spending or increase income without increasing expenses. If people do not plan and think they can accomplish complex goals without structure, they will likely not achieve them. Hold onto this conversation about strategy, as we will revisit it later in the solution chapters. Now, back to the environment.

## The Power of Environment

Most research and articles you will find address the issue of burnout from one angle. It acknowledges that pastors are burned out, and there is a growing trend. The research points to pastors in different denominations or reformations dealing with burnout. Then, they provide similar answers that are worded differently. The problem is that people often examine the research out of context, quoting the solutions without referencing all the academic parts, thereby ignoring the framework outlined by the writer. The process for understanding why pastors burn out can be addressed in a couple of ways.

In this book, we will look at one framework, and prayerfully, we will explore other methodologies in subsequent books and workshops. A framework is needed, similar to the guidance we use to engage scripture or the methods we should implore to communicate the Gospel. Frameworks provide steps so the reader can see how a person arrived at a solution. Education has changed so much over the years, though when I was in school, my math teachers always said, "Show your work." They did not want you to write the answer alone. They wanted to know how you arrived at that answer. The reason was that, depending on the problem, you could have taken the wrong steps and gotten the correct answer, you could have guessed, or, worse, you could have copied off your neighbor's worksheet. To better understand our paradox, we will use a framework that addresses the pastor, their environment, and their response (also known as behavior).

Social cognitive theory (SCT) focuses on the triadic interplay of the individual, behavior, and the environment.[12] Later in this chapter, the model shows the interaction between these three areas. These three areas can affect each other differently, and the relationship is not fixed. As noted in my research: *"A person can be conditioned to behavior due to constraints or consequences. A clergy member's conviction or goal will determine their behavior, affecting their environment. The process does not terminate but continues with each action affecting the other areas until the action is completed or abandoned."*
See figure 1 below.

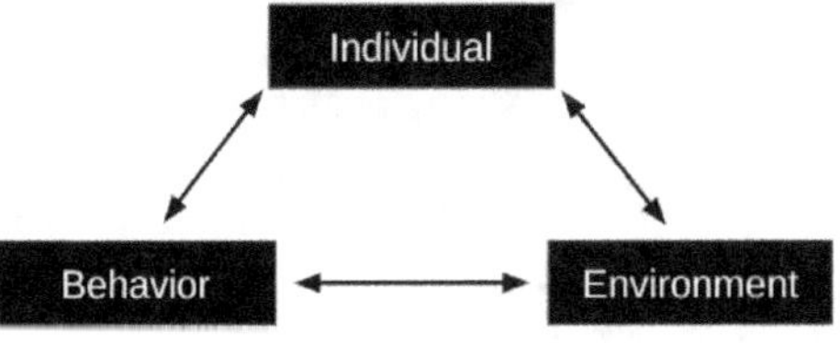


3

It is assumed that most people would linearly view their interaction. That calling, job, roles, and relationships converge with personal goals, identity, and ideals. As clergy members attempt to fulfill their duties, they face additional concerns, and attempts to master those concerns lead to burnout.

This linear view is not wrong. However, it ignores the dynamic interplay between these three areas. The convergence approach neglects the continuous interaction of the environment, the individual, and behavior, an essential function of SCT and understanding burnout. An individual's perception of the environment is often more important than reality.[4] Using SCT, we can focus on the pastor and the interplay within the individual as these various forces, responsibilities, and actions interact. We have historically looked at burnout with a focus on the pastor and behavior. The environment has been, in most cases, an afterthought.

So, we have not understood the view or the impact of the environment accurately, and we have minimized the environmental effect on pastors.

> We have historically looked at burnout with a focus on the pastor and behavior

People, not just pastors, have numerous external and internal forces prompting actions or behavior, even if we are unaware of these impulses. The external forces are not separate but interactive and interconnected within the environment.

As stated earlier, most interventions focus on the pastor making adjustments, yet the hidden factor is the environment. At the end of 2022, I listened to a webinar hosted by two pastors to discuss burnout and pastoral well-being. It was a positive session where they spoke and transparently shared what they had encountered related to burnout. Toward the end of the session, some general solutions were provided, primarily focused on the pastor. As leaders, we are taught to adapt to our environment, though sometimes we need to change our environment so it does not kill us. We will examine the environmental effect in the upcoming case study. The environment is formidable. The effect that the environment had on our nine pastors may surprise you. Our environment regularly controls us.

In our case study, you will see how the environment caused the pastors to make decisions that were not the best. Pastors (and people) are affected by their environment more than they think. If pastors want to change, yet the environment pushes them in an unhealthy direction, they will continue to make decisions that keep them in a place of burnout.

When a pastor is looking to address burnout, there should be no process that does not include at least one directive to assess their environment. This simple approach will challenge our faith because it seems "too practical," and we like radical faith. Though some of the "faith" we have been taught has been the basis for some pastors burning out. Pastors with large mortgages, extensive building projects, and community development initiatives may have the weekly burden of praying and believing God to send the resources to meet their needs. If we are honest, we have seen this as we look at how a consumer and social media-driven society pushes its will on the church and its leaders. Please understand that I am not saying that we should not have faith. We should believe God for great and mighty things, though we need to use wisdom to ensure that we are not getting into something that will bury us in the end.

## Chapter Reflections:

1. Have you ever considered how much your environment directs your decision-making?

2. Have you ever been sick on a Sunday and had to decide what to do? Did you preach or stay home? In hindsight, did you make the right decision? Why?

3. Are you a strategic or visionary leader? How has that style of leadership been to your advantage or disadvantage?

---

1. Bandura, A. (1977). Self-efficacy: Toward a unifying theory of behavioral change. Psychological Review, 84(2), 191–215. https://doi.org/10.1037/0033-295X.84.2.191

2. Bandura, A. (2018). Toward a psychology of human agency: Pathways and reflections. Perspectives on Psychological Science, 13(2), 130–136. https://doi.org/10.1177/1745691617699280

3. Adapted from "Social Cognitive Theory of Organizational Management," by R. Wood and A. Bandura, 1989, The Academy of Management, 14(3), p. 362. (https://doi.org/10.2307/258173)

4. Gardiner, H. W., & Kosmitzki, C. (2008). Lives across cultures: Cross-cultural human development (4th ed.). Pearson Allyn and Bacon.

---

"Of all men's miseries, the
bitterest is this: to know
so much and to have
control over nothing."

— Herodotus, Greek
Historian
(5th Century BC)

---

# 6

# CONTROL, COMMUNITY, COMPETENCY & COVID-19

One of the most frustrating moments as a human being is to have the desire or the opportunity to do something, yet not be able to do it. To be working in a job and know exactly how to solve the problem, yet because you are so low on the ladder, you are doing work that you know is not profitable. We start here because lack of control is a crucial component in our burnout conversation and connects to the person and the environment. Lack of control is about a person's schedule. A person constantly not knowing what the day will bring, not sure what will happen, or constantly having new problems or issues can lead to burnout and frustration over time. Pastoring can be unpredictable.

I have a good friend who is a pastor in the southern part of the United States. He was having a typical day until he heard the church was on fire.  Another pastor I know was on his way to minister and received a call that somebody had stolen the church van, went joy riding, and crashed it. Growing up, I remember somebody had broken into my home church and stolen the new computer from the church office. Pastors can have the most thought-out schedule or plan, and things can change within moments. A pastor usually has other priorities that need to be addressed, though, in the face of church situations, they will make the necessary adjustments to begin problem-solving the church's problem.

Control is paired with two other areas that are critical tenants of motivational theory. We will not exhaust all components of motivational theory. However, it should be noted that a lack of motivation or the introduction of certain activities over time will lead to burnout. Again, a framework helps guide the conversation so that we have something to anchor our thoughts to and can be solution-driven through the framework.

Burnout is cognitive, so these frameworks help us better understand how to combat it from the cognitive and learning sides

Burnout is cognitive, so these frameworks help us better understand how to combat it from the cognitive and learning sides. We will discuss control, community, and competency. Since we started the chapter with control, let us continue with it.

## Control

Control can also be experienced as autonomy. Lack of control will demotivate people over time. Understanding the effects of low control/autonomy is essential not only to pastors but also to the leaders they employ in ministry. Sincere leaders often struggle as the *hindered helper* in an environment built on unsustainable systems. The person who goes to work and has excellent ideas that are often dismissed or not encouraged will slowly lose motivation. Alternatively, if that same person were promised to lead a project, but each time the opportunity was taken away, that person would eventually become demotivated. As they continue to go to work, their motivation will diminish. The same is true for leaders. The problem pastors face is overcoming the feelings of being demotivated with the work they are called to lead; this continued position of stagnation (and frustration) will lead to burnout. Here is an excerpt from my research:[1234]

Autonomy focuses on "choice, acknowledgment of feelings, and opportunities for self-direction." When individuals cannot use their skills or make critical decisions related to career or work, it limits autonomy, demotivates, and can lead to burnout. A person's autonomy can be restricted if the job is unpredictable and demanding, making it hard to keep a schedule or plan actionable items for the day.

A leader may have a preferred outcome for an event, though they often cannot acknowledge their true feelings. So, that leader cannot always share how they honestly feel. Historically, pastors being transparent was almost taboo. Pastors were perceived in a particular manner, and sharing their problems or concerns from the pulpit was not encouraged. Currently, pastors want to share more, though there is a risk that the congregation will view them differently, and social media can make something small into something much more extensive (sound bites are dangerous). Pastors must be specific in their feelings (if they share them), not to create rumors or speculations. When a pastor says, "I am taking some time off", or the need arises to focus on personal matters, the accusations, and assumptions start to fly.

The other side is the need for the congregation to acknowledge the pastor's feelings without being told to do so. Here is an example: a pastor lost one of his parents. After the funeral, the following Sunday, they were back in the pulpit. With no prompting from the pastor, one of the leaders spoke to the congregation and asked them to give the pastor time. They encouraged the congregation to let him process all that had happened and not bombard him over the next few months. The individual elaborated on the church structure and told members to please utilize the other leaders during this time. The point is that that leader acknowledged the pastor's feelings without being prompted, which uplifts the pastor. However, if you have been pastoring for a while, you know the leader's plea fell on deaf ears for some, who still said they "had to speak to the pastor" when another leader could have handled the issue. Nevertheless, let us not dwell there – the environment we serve in can be unsympathetic to a pastor's circumstances.

Next, there is self-direction. Pastors may lack the ability to lead as they see fit or in the manner that they feel is best. Suppose a pastor's schedule is not constant. In that case, they do not have control over it to the degree they would like, and they cannot lead due to constraints, such as an oversight board, denominational edicts, or the congregation's desires. These conditions will lead them to burnout. Note that independent churches may not face the same pastoral constraints as pastors within the confines of a denomination. If the pastor is under a bishop, elder, or overseer who has a say in how they run their church, it can rob the pastor of self-direction.

Pastors are excited to share God's word and to see people grow. They have a vision for the church and often, through prayer and time with God, have a path for guiding people to spiritual maturity. Pastoring becomes laborious when they cannot put any of that into practice. Note: we are not discussing accountability or spiritual guidance when referring to institutional constraints. These constraints are similar to micromanaging the pastor on every church component, so they have no room to breathe or operate as the pastor. Pastors in full-time ministry are often at the mercy of denominational leadership or an oversight board.

Some pastors have walked into situations where the people do not want to change and have the authority to vote or put the pastor out. The congregation wants the pastor to preach on Sunday and do a Bible study on Wednesday, and that is it. They are not interested in transformation or change. This level of restricted mundane activity will also burn a pastor out. One additional area that can push pastors further into burnout is finances. When pastors cannot control the financial flow of the church, this is to say that when a pastor is not sure what the church's finances will look like from week to week, that can be a source of burnout. Will people give? Will we have enough to pay the bills or do other activities? Having this financial conversation can aid in pushing a pastor further into burnout. As a pastor, how much control do you currently have? Is it enough? What area do you wish you had a better handle on? Before we transition to the next section, take a minute and actually reflect on these questions.

## Community

The idea of community can also be labeled as belongingness or relatedness.[5] I have personally seen more pastors focusing on their personal community, which is encouraging. Note that the focus is on the need to be connected, not the issue of loneliness. Since pastors and clergy have a calling, it can be assumed that they do not need motivation or this "community" to walk with them. We have all heard that sometimes you must walk alone, or sometimes you have to be willing to do it by yourself.

> "...the focus is on the need to be connected, not the issue of loneliness."

This ideology is true, yet the Bible cautions us that being alone is a dangerous place to find yourself. The writer of Ecclesiastes 4:9-10 (KJV) states, *"Two are better than one; because they have a good reward for their labour. For if they fall, the one will lift up his fellow: but woe to him that is alone when he falleth; for he hath not another to help him up."* So, pastors need this sense of belonging. Historically, one of the reasons we may not have seen this emphasized as much is that most of the research we see on burnout is data from within large denominations. Denominations, by default, have a built-in community component. We now have more independent, non-denominational churches. The belonging component is not automatic and must be fostered.

Belongingness is a tenet that is critical for pastors, even those in denominations, since being connected can reduce burnout. Operating as an island is harmful; it is a factor in burnout among pastors and undermines their ability to be fully functional in their work. Isolated leadership harms the individual, especially when working in a demanding environment. Pastors suffer from burnout caused by being disconnected and working in a challenging environment. For many of them, their daily actions are directly connected to the individuals they lead, which can be unpredictable.[6,7,8,9]

Let me also say it can be hard to find somebody you can trust, period. Finding someone you can trust is hard for leaders, pastors, and most individuals. Given their position, pastors may find it challenging (or unwise) to share their troubles, issues, concerns, or even moments of lacking faith. We all go through problematic seasons though many believe pastors do not face similar problems.

Pastors have to find another pastor or person that they trust. If the person is not a professional counselor or therapist, then the person(s) must be able to hear where the pastor is and not diminish God's call on their life. They <u>must</u> be able to hear, provide sound guidance if needed, and be confidential. People like this are hard to find. Especially if you are a well-known pastor, some entities will pay large sums of money to get "dirt" on prominent people. Which is a sad but true reality that pastors must face.

## Competency

There are different ways to approach competency. Based on our framework, we will define it as a person's "capacity to interact effectively with their environment."[10] Lack of results affects pastors. When pastors have nothing to point to as growth or accomplishment, it can cause a problem. People talk about not caring about the size of their church or having a larger building, which may be accurate, but it does not mean that lack of church growth does not affect them. Those things matter, especially if the pastor is not seeing progress in other areas. When people cannot achieve their goals, they will subconsciously question if they have the "competency" to do the work.

Here is the challenge with pastors versus other helping professionals. Pastors have many roles, and competency becomes a focal point because not all pastors have the experience or education to perform some of them.

In the article "Addressing pastoral knowledge and attitudes about clergy/mental health practitioner collaboration," the researchers note that a lack of results and feelings of inadequacy will lead to burnout. Most pastors do not enter pastoring to be fundraisers, project managers, mediators, accountants, and budget directors, though many have to wear those hats. Consider this: Even pastors who thrive on challenges, not achieving goals or having results plateau can cause them to question their ability for the position and limit motivation. 11121314

Most pastors do not enter pastoring to be fundraisers, project managers, mediators, accountants, and budget directors...

The main issue for pastors during the COVID-19 pandemic was that these three areas were put into play simultaneously, without warning, and at high speed. Regardless of what you did as a pastor or your thoughts about the pandemic, we can all agree that it changed the world we live in and the dynamics of the church.

## COVID-19 (a perfect storm)

COVID-19 was all three areas coming together and hitting pastors simultaneously, though most pastors did not know it. This section will serve as a mini case study because COVID-19 pushed all the red buttons, and the church went into a tailspin. Remember, each of these three areas will push a person into burnout.

First, let us address control. Nobody had control throughout the pandemic. The churches did not know how long it would last, guidance was constantly changing, and there were a lot of new hats pastors had to start wearing. Most pastors had to deal with the death of members, many impromptu meetings, and navigating the unknown in their personal lives in conjunction with the church. How many videos did we see with Pastors trying to conduct Bible Study or Sunday Service from their house, and they were interrupted? The kids entered the room, the dog started barking, or somebody started yelling and did not realize the pastor was recording. I remember I spoke for a couple of church services during the pandemic. I am thankful they were only conference calls with no video because I preached from inside the car and the garage to reduce the likelihood of being unintentionally interrupted.

Pastors were also not sure about their finances. Sadly, several churches lost their buildings due to the lost of control in generating funds. People had other priorities, individuals lost their jobs, and so much occurred that the church suffered financially. Again, not all churches, but not having control over the finances and the uncertainty of the moment pushed many pastors down a road facing burnout. That level of unpredictability for an undisclosed amount of time in multiple areas led to burnout.

Second was the lack of community. This one will vary, but the usual interactions such as conferences, convocations, meetings, and gatherings did not occur. People were confined to their homes, and all their interactions had to be initially via phone or video. Many pastors confessed that they did not realize that all these other pastors felt the same way. They thought it was only them. Many pastors went into isolation during this time, not intentionally, as they focused on how to keep their church going forward. So, the community became less of a priority and helped move them closer to burnout. Again, COVID-19 was a perfect storm; the three major areas that lead to burnout were placed on the shoulders of pastors, and most had no idea why they were feeling the way they were. The hope is that pastors can avoid entering burnout, though if you do burn out, there is a path back to a place of balance.

The third area is competency. Competency is where most pastors experience pressure and problems. During the COVID-19 pandemic, pastors had to move to a hybrid or online version of church. Pastors stated that they felt as if they were more tired even though they may have been doing less work preaching or teaching online. The issue there was competency. Most pastors had never used those online platforms until the pandemic. For example, I used Zoom for two years before the pandemic. Most people were not using Zoom or were even familiar with the platform. So, people's fatigue was related to competency, the ability to interact with their environment. The environment was now virtual. So, in the beginning, pastors were trying to control everything on Zoom, creating a cognitive strain.

Next, some pastors were uncomfortable preaching from their desks or leading worship from their living rooms. All pastors knew how to preach. It was preaching from a new setup, with no real interaction, just you, the pastor, a screen, and a microphone. That was different.  Third, some pastors moved back into the sanctuary yet had to acclimate to preaching in an empty room. There are some messages; if you go back and listen, you can hear the echo in the sanctuary but understand it was not an easy transition.

Lastly, for the churches that had dedicated audio, visual, and sound staff, the pastors did not have to worry about becoming an expert in those areas. Having a tech team to delegate to was an invaluable gift to pastors who were so positioned. Not all churches have dedicated media staff, so it became a burden on the pastor, who now had to wear the hat of a sound technician and visual director. This created a two-fold problem for these pastors. Working to operate and grow a new skill in A/V production, coupled with the mental strain of not knowing how long they would have to operate in a virtual space, led to burnout. If some leaders knew they would have to operate in that manner for four months, they would have been fine. The ambiguity of not knowing is what exacerbated this issue. The long-term effect in this post-pandemic world is that society as a whole is more equipped than ever to accommodate a virtual experience. Now pastors wrestle with the divide between people who want to stay virtual and those who want to be back in the church. So many churches still maintain an online presence because they do not want to lose those members who wish to stay virtual. The issue is that pastors have fewer people in the church building to assist and serve, which limits productivity.

COVID-19 shook the church and forced pastors to engage at levels they were not expecting. Many pastors burned out, and even post-pandemic pastors still feel the residual effects.

**_Knowledge Point:_** A lack of control, community, or competency will lead to burnout.  The more of these components that are missing, the faster the pastor will find themselves headed to burnout.

After this case study, we will head toward our solutions to get each pastor some tools to fight burnout as you lead your church.

# Chapter Reflections:

1. As a pastor what are some areas that you hoped you had more control over?

2. Reflecting on the community around you as a pastor, is your community sufficient, or do you perceive that there are deficiencies? If there are deficiencies, what do you need to improve or change?

3. How have you or other pastors increased competency in areas that you were not fully equipped to operate in as a pastor?

4. Based on your observation, what is the most damaging effect that COVID-19 has had on the church and pastors?

---

1. Washington, B. (2021). Understanding Burnout in Non-denominational Clergy: A Social Cognitive Approach (Doctoral dissertation, University of Southern California).

2. Ryan, R., & Deci, E. (2000b). Self-determination theory and the facilitation of intrinsic motivation, social development, and well-being. The American Psychologist, 55(1), 68–78. https://doi.org/10.1037/0003-066X.55.1.68

3. Leiter, M.P., & Maslach, C. (2017). Motivation, competence and job burnout. In A. J. Elliot, C. S. Dweck, & D. S. Yeager (Eds.), Handbook of competence and motivation (2nd ed., pp. 370–384). The Guilford Press.

4. Lee, C., & Rosales, A. (2020). Self-regard in pastoral ministry: Self-compassion versus self-criticism in a sample of United Methodist clergy. Journal of Psychology and Theology, 48(1), 18–33. https://doi.org/10.1177/0091647119870290

5. Ryan, R., & Deci, E. (2000a). Intrinsic and extrinsic motivations: Classic definitions and new directions. Contemporary Educational Psychology, 25(1), 54–67. https://doi.org/10.1006/ceps.1999.1020

6. Washington, B. (2021). Understanding Burnout in Non-denominational Clergy: A Social Cognitive Approach (Doctoral dissertation, University of Southern California).

7. Lee, C., & Rosales, A. (2020). Self-regard in pastoral ministry: Self-compassion versus self-criticism in a sample of United Methodist clergy. Journal of Psychology and Theology, 48(1), 18–33. https://doi.org/10.1177/0091647119870290

8. Scott, G., & Lovell, R. (2015). The rural pastors initiative: Addressing isolation and burnout in rural ministry. Pastoral Psychology, 64(1), 71–97. https://doi.org/10.1007/s11089-013-0591-z

9. Warner, J., & Carter, J. D. (1984). Loneliness, marital adjustment and burnout in pastoral and lay persons. Journal of Psychology and Theology, 12(2), 125–131. https://doi.org/10.1177/009164718401200206

10. Ryan, R. M., & Moller, A. C. (2017). Competence as central, but not sufficient, for high-quality motivation. In A.J. Elliot, C.S. Dweck & D.S. Yeager (Eds.) Handbook of competence and motivation: Theory and application (2nd ed., pp. 216–238). The Guildford Press.

11. Washington, B. (2021). Understanding Burnout in Non-denominational Clergy: A Social Cognitive Approach (Doctoral dissertation, University of Southern California).

12. Barnard, L.K., & Curry, J.F. (2012). The relationship of clergy burnout to self-compassion and other personality dimensions. Pastoral Psychology, 61(2), 149–163. https://doi.org/10.1007/s11089-011-0377-0

13. Pines, A. M. (1993). Burnout: An existential perspective. In W.M. Schaufeli & C. Maslach (Eds.), Professional burnout (1st ed., pp. 33–51). Routledge. https//doi.org/10.4324/9781315227979

14. Ryan, R. M., & Moller, A. C. (2017). Competence as central, but not sufficient, for high-quality motivation. In A.J. Elliot, C.S. Dweck & D.S. Yeager (Eds.) Handbook of competence and motivation: Theory and application (2nd ed., pp. 216–238). The Guildford Press.

"People exercise an
unconscious selection in
being influenced."

— T.S. Eliot

# 7

# CASE STUDY – ENVIRONMENT

As we explored in chapters 4 and 5, the environment plays a massive part in how a pastor can address burnout. People have ignored burnout because we have equated no longer feeling tired with overcoming burnout. To that end, time away, as we stated before, will reduce tiredness and mental fatigue, all of which are a part of the final solution. Again, referring to our early chapters, if the issue is the pastor's work schedule and they can control all aspects of the schedule, then personal adjustments can mitigate burnout. For example, if the pastor is a workaholic or wants to please everyone, they can make personal changes to tackle burnout. However, if the causes of burnout are a combination of the pastor's personal choices and the environment around them, more will have to be done to address burnout.

The pastors in our study all agree that vacations or sabbaticals are good practices. However, this is the issue of environment and how a pastor's environment can hinder what the pastor knows is best practice. Before we make pastors the anomaly, this is human nature.

Consider the person who has sick days, yet the boss or company "needs them to be in the office," so they still go in to work because of the company culture. Our environment plays a significant role in our decision-making, and it is a concept that we all can learn from, not only leaders. When I worked in consulting, people often said, "Culture will eat your strategy for breakfast." This statement meant that no amount of good processes, standard operating procedures, or other internal strategies could out perform an organization's prevailing behavior. If the company's culture is antithetical to the leader's vision, all the good intensions will be devoured, and any noticeable change will be for the worst.

Pastor Conner did not negate the need for time away, though he acknowledged that sometimes circumstances or letting go are not as simplistic.

## Pastor Conner

I feel strongly about vacations, but I'm not good at taking them. I believe my church is not far enough along for me to leave them for an extended period. I am just being honest; things would go haywire without me. I am, however, convicted. It is a growth opportunity for me, and I am making progress in accepting that I must take time away from the church. I believe it is vital because it models Jesus. Jesus would do ministry and then retreat. The need for a vacation or time away is significant. However, there are reasons that pastors, myself included, use to justify not taking a vacation.

Let us look at the environment's effect on what was shared. Pastor Conner knows that vacations or time away are helpful. However, looking at his environment, which is his church, he does not feel that they would function well without him. That could be seen as a personal conflict within himself, though in reality, his environment is not at a level that allows him to walk away, so even though it is best practice, he does not do it. Conjoined to this is that many people have to make the mental decision to step away, whether for a short vacation or a more extended sabbatical. It is one thing to be away from the church, and it is another thing to be away and take your hands off the steering wheel. Many pastors step away, though they keep their hands on the steering wheel, defeating the purpose of the time away. Again, this is no different than the business professional who stays glued to their work email even while they are on the beach for a family vacation. So, pastors are not unique in this area.

Pastor Nathan shared that taking time off to address burnout can be a question of control, and past that point, the decision has to be a joint effort between the leader and the church.

## Pastor Nathan

> I think control is one issue. Leaving the church to somebody else or others while you are completely unplugged from it for a few weeks is frightening to some people. You are used to being involved in everything, knowing all the decisions, and people

are used to seeing you. Also, the financial component is a big part not often discussed. The church has to agree that if the pastor takes a sabbatical, this person will not be "working" for three months, and we will still pay them. That does not always go over well with people. I think that is probably the most significant driver because you and the church have to partner and understand the importance of your being away.

Pastor Nathan covers two issues: control and partnership. Let us focus on partnership first.  The congregation has to support a pastor who is taking time away. That is a substantial environmental factor. The congregation must align with the pastor who needs that time away, not only to address burnout but also for normality. Pastors can seem superhuman, though most do not try to portray themselves as superheroes. Pastors are humans, and a vacation is something that they should take, not because they are burned out or fighting depression. We all need a moment in our lives when we can relax and have minimal responsibilities. Pastor Nathan states that if a pastor wants to be on sabbatical for an extended time, the congregation must support it. It may sound simple, but we know that not all churches are created equal, and some churches will argue against a sabbatical, which is another story.

Then, Pastor Nathan mentioned control. Whether we agree or not, control is essential. Managing and taking care of your congregation as a pastor is crucial. If you have been in church long enough, you have attended at least one church service and raised an eyebrow during the worship experience (be honest). Pastors know that giving some people the microphone is an opportunity for some people to go off the rails, especially if the leader is not in the building.

> Managing and taking care of your congregation as a pastor is crucial

Now, people will counter with, "That is why training is important," for which I agree. Training, however, is only as good as the people available to the leader. Some people will still find a way to end up in the wrong place, no matter how you train them. Read that again slowly. Remember, a pastor can only utilize what is available to them; in some cases, the unpredictable ones are the only people available or willing to serve. I digress. Let us examine this more closely based on our earlier framework, which looks at the interaction between the individual, environment, and behavior. The pastor knows that vacations are good. However, because of environmental constraints, they do not take a vacation. So, a pastor can know what needs to be done. However, an environmental construct may persuade them to do something different.

Let us continue the conversation. Some pastors are not constrained by the environment as much as their beliefs constrain them. So, their convictions constrain them. The pastor agrees that vacations or sabbaticals are good. However, they internally choose to continue in ministry even when burned out because of what they have seen in ministry (we call this modeling). The environment, in this case, is not the cause. The internal calibration of the individual pushes their behavior in a direction opposite to what they know is right.

Some pastors acknowledged the need for a vacation or a break and spoke about cultural trends, growing up in church, and how what they saw as kids and early in ministry shaped how they viewed vacations or sabbaticals. The idea that the pastor would not be at church because they were on vacation was not the standard, as some participants recall from growing up in church. Pastor Julius explained that the pastor was always in church and, to a fault, modeled their behavior of not taking vacations.

## Pastor Julius

In my experience growing up, it was my understanding that as a pastor, your job was to teach and preach, period. There is no such thing as "taking a break." You take a break when God calls you home. When you die, you can rest. That is your break; that is your reward. Until then, you do everything you can to push through so things can get done and God can get the glory.

Pastor Ryan spoke about growing up in church and a similar conviction that the church pastor followed.

## Pastor Ryan

I grew up in a tradition where the pastor never took a vacation. They were in church every week to preach. My mindset over the years has changed to the point where I believe we must retreat. A term often used in scripture, "Selah," means to pause. So, there are moments when we have to pause, reflect, or step away. So, I believe in vacations.

These two examples show that burnout again is more than just walking away for a few weeks. There are steps and cognitive actions that occur that even when a pastor wants to do the right thing or has the mind to do what is best, there are factors that they may not be aware of that can cause them to choose a less optimal option.

Let us continue to talk. Now, we have heard conversations about vacations and sabbaticals. However, what happens if a person does not even realize that they need to step away or vacations were not a part of their life experiences? Remember, pastors are an amazingly dynamic group. Pastors are in urban, suburban, and rural areas, some with 15 members and some with 15,000 members. All of them are pastors. We cannot assume that they all view life the same or have had the same life experiences.

In some cases, pastors do not always realize the need to get away. It was not based on a model or a need to control; it was just not a priority on their radar. Pastor Daniel spoke candidly about being in ministry and then becoming a pastor and how the need to get away was much more significant and was not an ideal that he focused on before pastoring.

## Pastor Daniel

We are in denial. We do not even realize that the battery is about to die, and we are trying to get somewhere. When I was ordained, one of the pastors who laid hands on me said, sometimes, brother, you will have to steal away. I did not understand what that meant. As I started pastoring, I realized what he was saying. So, now I take vacations.

Similarly, Pastor Esther shared that it was not until her first vacation that vacations became a priority.

## Pastor Esther

The first actual vacation I went on was 2 or 3 years ago when I took the family to Disney World. I was able to relax with my family and do nothing. It was a mental break from worrying about church or work. Vacations are necessary because if I am not at work or church, I am at home, and when I am at home, I do not relax. So, getting away and taking a break from everything is heaven on earth.

When the pastors took a break, they noticed that vacations are needed, and it is a practice that they should conscientiously incorporate into their lives. Pastor Michael agreed with this and shared the benefit of going on vacation with consideration for their specific church.

## Pastor Michael

I do not think that vacations are a bad idea at all. Vacations have never been practical for us, but that does not mean that pastors should not get away. We went on a vacation a couple of years ago. Much of our time was spent eating and taking afternoon naps because you realize you do not know how physically tired you are.

As much as this conversation is about the environment, it is also about knowledge. The more we know about burnout, the better we can combat it. All these moving parts in our lives have varying effects and can lead us to burn out or away from what is essential. No pastor intends to burn out; some pastors will never encounter burnout.

> The more we know about burnout, the better we can combat it

As the church experience continues to change and we enter into new areas of ministry to reach the world with the Gospel, pastors will be prone to burnout. In the following chapters, we will begin providing solutions to mitigate burnout. The burnout conversation is vast, so these are the primary responses drawn from research.

# Chapter Reflections:

1. What areas in your current environment do you need to re-evaluate?

2. Do you agree with these pastors? Why or why not?

3. Why do you think so few people examine their environment when considering burnout?

4. Do you feel that you have control over your environment, or does it push you in a direction you do not want to go?

––––––––

"It is not the answer that
enlightens, but the
question."

-Eugene Ionesco.


"Millions saw the apple
fall, but Newton was the
one who asked why."

-Bernard Baruch

––––––––

# 8

# Is This Burnout or Compassion Fatigue?

As our entire conversation has focused on burnout, there is a question we need to ask. I encourage you to ask yourself, "Based on what I have read, am I dealing with burnout?" The reason for this question is that other conditions can mirror burnout. I will briefly discuss those in this chapter and suggest you speak to a counselor or therapist if unsure. Remember, we are not directly diagnosing you. We are examining the reasons pastors burn out through a learning, academic, and cognitive lens. So, if you feel as if you are burned out based on what you have read, be sure to speak with your doctor, a counselor, or a therapist.  You want to ensure that you are dealing with burnout only and not with burnout *plus* another concern.

The other conditions have different triggers, and the solutions are also different.  For example, a pastor could be facing burnout and anxiety.  In that case, these steps will often help with burnout, though a medical professional may need to prescribe additional interventions or medication to address the anxiety.  My goal, prayer, and intent are for pastors to operate optimally to fulfill the goals and mandates that God has given them.  A burned-out pastor will not make it to the end of the race.

> A burned-out pastor will not make it to the end of the race

The Apostle Paul writes in 2 Timothy 4:6-7, *"For I am now ready to be offered, and the time of my departure is at hand. I have fought a good fight, I have finished my course, I have kept the faith."* The enemy's use of burnout prevents pastors from "finishing their course." Some pastors today have left the ministry, not because they were finished but because they were fatigued. Such findings are not meant to be a judgment but an observation. In order to continue in life and move forward, these leaders felt it best to leave or resign from ministry. Most of them did not want to leave. However, once they'd reached such a critical stage of fatigue, stepping away was the only option they felt remained.

Many of them are hurt, bitter, and even resentful toward God. The struggle of those who chose to walk away is not a matter of eternal life but eternal reward. Some would honestly confess that they fear ultimately learning that they did not finish their course. Again, this is not a judgment but a reality of the enemy's strategy to derail our ministry, removing us from an aspect of our race. Yes, we can still live for Christ and do other things, but it will be hard to fulfill the call outside of the pastoral position if the call is to be a pastor.

In the dialog about burnout, we must remember that every condition is not burnout. Seasonal Depression (Seasonal Affective Disorder) can resemble burnout. The symptoms related to this disorder, as provided by the Mayo Clinic, can mirror burnout symptoms.[1] The difference is the trigger. Seasonal Affective Disorder is connected to changes in the seasons, which is different from the causes we have discussed related to burnout.

Connected to pastors and burnout is the issue of compassion fatigue. Many pastors will or have experienced compassion fatigue and may not have been aware of how closely it mirrors burnout. The two conditions are different, yet the effect can be similar. *The Journal of Psychology and Theology* defines Compassion Fatigue, also known as Secondary Traumatic Stress, as "An emotional state in which an individual surrenders to and is moved by the emotional experiences of others."[2]

The symptoms of compassion fatigue can resemble burnout. They include but are not limited to, exhaustion, disrupted sleep, anxiety, headaches, stomach upset, irritability, numbness, a decreased sense of purpose, and emotional disconnection.[3]

Other issues, ailments, and conditions resemble burnout or can operate in tandem with burnout, as was mentioned earlier with burnout and anxiety. If a pastor is unsure, they are encouraged to seek medical assistance to ensure they are addressing the correct concern.

Though our conversation is about burnout, I need to focus for a minute on compassion fatigue. Dr. Christina Maslach is one of the leading academics regarding burnout. She has a book titled *Burnout: The Cost of Caring*. Pastors are responsible for caring for their congregation, and a cost is associated with that level of care. Caring is not free. There is a cost, a heavy cost associated with caring. This "cost" is the reason for focusing on compassion fatigue. Most people, me included, do not spend enough time considering the cost of caring for or assisting others.

> There is a cost, a heavy cost associated with caring

Everyone has a personal *caring account*; this is the amount of caring you can optimally provide. Once you exhaust your ability to care, you risk falling into compassion fatigue. Everyone's caring account has a different capacity, and it can be difficult to tell when your account is becoming depleted. Let us take this one step further. The cost of caring is like a toll; in economic terms, a toll is another word for a tax. When an individual drives on a road with a toll, they are essentially being taxed for using that road. The same is true for us as humans and even more for pastors. Every time a pastor shows up for a funeral, answers the phone call of a distressed member, visits a hospitalized person, has a counseling session, or even writes a letter to an incarcerated member, there is a toll assessed on their "caring account."

I grew up in the Northeastern part of the US, and we had plenty of tolls. You paid tolls once you left Connecticut, heading south on Interstate 95. The tolls I remember were The New Jersey Turnpike, all the bridges or tunnels in New York, the Garden State Parkway, and the Delaware Memorial Bridge. Growing up, my parents had to stop at the toll booths and physically pay each of those tolls. Some tolls had a fixed price, and others changed based on the distance you drove on the road. Nevertheless, as a driver, you were very aware of the amount of money you spent traveling from point A to point B because of the physical exchange of the money.

Now, with technology, you have a toll transponder (wireless transmitter) in your car, and you do not stop; you drive through the toll booths, and it records the toll amount and charges it to your account. If the individual does not check their account, they will not know how much they have paid for each toll. In addition, if a person is not careful, they can go into the negative because they have gone through more tolls than the amount of money in their account. Due to technology (emails, cell phones, text messages, social media, and video conferencing), many pastors are paying tolls that they may not even be aware of, rapidly depleting their "caring accounts."

We must also realize that we do not have separate *caring accounts* for our personal lives. Let me say that, again, pastors do not have separate *caring accounts* for their personal lives. The caring account a pastor uses for the church is the same one they will draw from for their personal life. So, if they deplete all their caring attending to the church, they will have nothing left for their family or close friends.

### *Knowledge Point:*

Compassion is a limited resource.

Leaders are solicited to address multiple issues and concerns, so they are susceptible to burnout and can experience compassion fatigue. Again, compassion fatigue is "an emotional state in which an individual surrenders to and is moved by the emotional experiences of others."[4] Compassion fatigue differs from burnout in that it can materialize immediately after a traumatic incident, whereas burnout occurs over time.[5] Compassion fatigue, initially called secondary traumatic stress, is often seen in individuals helping people deal with trauma or traumatic situations.

So, the trauma is not the pastors, though they experience the weight of it as they are helping their parishioners through their situation.[6] Think of it like secondhand smoke. I am not the one smoking, but because of my proximity to you as you smoke, I am negatively affected by it.

> Compassion fatigue differs from burnout in that it can materialize immediately

In the article "The Unseen Cost: A Discussion of the Secondary Traumatization Experience of the Clergy," the writers note that clergy are often the first and sometimes only individuals people turn to and trust when facing traumatic problems.[7] They help congregants manage death, abuse, domestic violence, infidelity, suicide, and other traumatic situations.[8] [9] Figley noted that "there is a cost to caring," and many pastors will suffer from compassion fatigue in exchange for assisting congregants who experience tragedy or trauma.[10] They often assist in "highly emotional" work such as officiating funerals and grief counseling.[11] Pastors must remember that compassion is a limited resource![12]

Compassion fatigue and burnout could have similar outcomes, yet different events precipitate each.[13] Burnout is usually a process related to the work a person is obligated to perform. Compassion fatigue is associated with assisting another person through a traumatic experience, and exposure to that traumatic incident leads to compassion fatigue. The research explains that "professionals who experience compassion fatigue feel overwhelmed, whereas professionals who experience burnout feel overworked."[14] In an article from the *Journal of Spirituality in Clinical Practice,* the researchers found that formal training related to compassion fatigue could help reduce its prevalence.

The study found that more than 75% of military psychologists who received formal training related to compassion fatigue did not develop it after assisting soldiers through traumatic situations.[15] In a 2020 article, Barna Group noted that 73% of the pastors surveyed felt "somewhat equipped" to help members dealing with various forms of trauma. Compassion fatigue could be a precursor to burnout, but researchers point out that an individual experiencing compassion fatigue will recover faster than a person who is burned out.[16] Pastors are special leaders whom people seek out during difficult times. As noted above, their work is mentally and physically demanding, and constant exposure to other people's trauma will, over time, affect their well-being.[17] [18] [19]

Compassion fatigue and burnout are the costs of working with people. The process of helping to grow people is expensive. No different than a physician who has to work with an uncooperative patient. People are a lot to handle.

## The Need For Results

Now, at the risk of burning you out (pun intended), we need to quickly revisit an earlier conversation from chapter six, namely results. There is nothing more frustrating than working hard and seeing no results. Results are important. In almost all areas of our life, we look for results. People want to see results when they change their workout habits or diet. They want to see weight loss or muscle gain. In other words, they want visible evidence that affirms what they are doing is working.

Researchers Leiter and Maslach note that a person's vocation often occupies a large portion of an individual's life with very few substitutes.[20] So, if a person or, in this case, a pastor is not successful in their job, almost no activities or events can substantially address the void that comes from this deficiency. Pastors will burn out when they do not see results.

If we think about our Christian experience, we "look back" at what God has done in our lives, and it provides confidence and motivation for us to trust Him with whatever we are currently facing. The more a person succeeds or has successful moments early in their endeavors, the more they will believe that they can produce the proper future outcomes.

Researcher Albert Bandura stated, "Success builds a robust belief in one's personal efficacy. Failure undermines it."[21] Self-efficacy is the idea that a person "can successfully execute the behavior required to produce the desired outcomes," as noted by Bandura in one of his classic articles.[22] One of the main elements of individuals being motivated or achieving success is their belief that they can produce a desired outcome. Even if there are other elements at work, a person has to believe that they can produce a specific outcome; if not, they will not be motivated to act or endure hardship.[23]

The key here is that results, success, or "wins" are essential in any leader's life, including pastors. Motivation can be increased in a few ways, though none of them equal to personally producing results. The following conversation around motivation is drawn from Bandura's article in the *Psychological Review* journal and provides powerful insight into how people are or are not motivated.[24] For example, a pastor can be motivated by another pastor building an edifice or paying off their mortgage. That vicarious experience will provide some motivation, though over time if the pastor does not achieve their own results, their motivation will fade.

In addition, verbal encouragement can build motivation. A person who receives verbal encouragement or feedback often believes they can achieve the desired goal. Suggestion is a strong influencer and can persuade pastors that they can be successful even if they were not successful in the past. However, motivation will only increase moderately or minimally because this form of encouragement is not greater than mastery or personal accomplishment. The effects of this form of encouragement can be easily "extinguished by disconfirming experiences."[25]

A pastor may be attempting to increase attendance at the church; however, initial attempts have failed or yielded poor results. Verbal encouragement from the congregation could lift the pastor's belief that increasing attendance is possible. The problem arises if the pastor continues and is met with defeat. Over time, those encouraging words will not be adequate because of the lack of results. A pastor has the added benefit of faith, which may help when conjoined with verbal encouragement, though lack of results over an extended time can be hard to overcome.

In some aspects of church achievement, God controls those results. Pastors cannot make people accept Christ or make people change. The reason for the last section of this chapter is that once a pastor sees that they are burning out, they must determine the cause. In many cases, having no results is why pastors burn out. A pastor leading a church for eight years and not seeing any definitive results in the last five years will take a toll on that pastor. Not all pastors are the same, and the results or lack thereof will affect them differently. However, when there are no results, no matter how much the congregation supports and encourages them, those words eventually lose their effect. *It does not matter how many pastors around you are succeeding; at some point, you will no longer see the success in the Body of Christ as encouraging; it can become discouraging.*

Pastors must determine if they are facing burnout or some other issue, and the impact of results cannot be ignored. The same is true with other helping professionals. If a person has no results, it will negatively impact them and may lead those individuals to burn out over time.

> It does not matter how many pastors around you are succeeding, at some you will no longer see the success in the Body of Christ as encouraging, it can become discouraging

# Chapter Reflections:

1. Before reading this chapter, were you aware of the difference between burnout and compassion fatigue?

2. Reflecting on your time as a pastor, are there times you labeled yourself stressed or burned out, and it may have been compassion fatigue?

4. Think of a time when you achieved something as a pastor that dramatically impacted your overall mood, attitude, and demeanor.

5. Do you feel that results are that important? Or can a pastor continue to lead with minimal results?

---

1. https://www.mayoclinic.org/diseases-conditions/seasonal-affective-disorder/symptoms-causes/syc-20364651

2. Snelgar, R. J., Renard, M., & Shelton, S. (2017). Preventing compassion fatigue amongst pastors: The influence of spiritual intelligence and intrinsic motivation. Journal of Psychology and Theology, 45(4), 247–260. https://doi.org/10.1177/009164711704500401

3. https://www.psychologytoday.com/us/basics/compassion-fatigue

4. Snelgar, R. J., Renard, M., & Shelton, S. (2017). Preventing compassion fatigue amongst pastors: The influence of spiritual intelligence and intrinsic motivation. Journal of Psychology and Theology, 45(4), 247–260.

5. Conrad, D., & Kellar-Guenther, Y. (2006). Compassion fatigue, burnout, and compassion satisfaction among colorado child protection workers. Child Abuse & Neglect, 30(10), 1071–1080. https://doi.org/10.1016/j.chiabu.2006.03.009

6. Figley, C. R. (1995). Compassion fatigue: Coping with secondary traumatic stress disorder in those who treat the traumatized. Routledge. https://doi.org/10.4324/9780203777381

7. Hendron, J. A., Irving, P., & Taylor, B. (2011). The unseen cost: A discussion of the secondary traumatization experience of the clergy. Pastoral Psychology, 61(2), 221–231. https://doi.org/10.1007/s11089-011-0378-z

8. Hendron, J. A., Irving, P., & Taylor, B. (2011). The unseen cost: A discussion of the secondary traumatization experience of the clergy. Pastoral Psychology, 61(2), 221–231. https://doi.org/10.1007/s11089-011-0378-z

9. Jacobson, J. M., Rothschild, A., Mirza, F., & Shapiro, M. (2013). Risk for burnout and compassion fatigue and potential for compassion satisfaction among clergy: Implications for social work and religious organizations. Haworth Press.

10. Figley, C. R. (1995). Compassion fatigue: Coping with secondary traumatic stress disorder in those who treat the traumatized. Routledge. https://doi.org/10.4324/9780203777381

11. Adams, C. J., Hough, H., Proeschold-bell, R. J., Yao, J., & Kolkin, M. (2017). Clergy burnout: A comparison study with other helping professions. Pastoral Psychology, 66(2), 147–175. https://doi.org/10.1007/s11089-016-0722-4

12. Snelgar, R. J., Renard, M., & Shelton, S. (2017). Preventing compassion fatigue amongst pastors: The influence of spiritual intelligence and intrinsic motivation. Journal of Psychology and Theology, 45(4), 247–260. https://doi.org/10.1177/009164711704500401

13. Udipi, S., Veach, P. M., Kao, J., & Leroy, B. S. (2008). The psychic costs of empathic engagement: Personal and demographic predictors of genetic counselor compassion fatigue. Journal of Genetic Counseling, 17(5), 459–471. https://doi.org/10.1007/s10897-008-9162-3

14. Udipi, S., Veach, P. M., Kao, J., & Leroy, B. S. (2008). The psychic costs of empathic engagement: Personal and demographic predictors of genetic counselor compassion fatigue. Journal of Genetic Counseling, 17(5), 459–471. https://doi.org/10.1007/s10897-008-9162-3

15. Noullet, C. J., Lating, J. M., Kirkhart, M. W., Dewey, R., & Everly, G. S., Jr. (2018). Effect of pastoral crisis intervention training on resilience and compassion fatigue in clergy: A pilot study. Spirituality in Clinical Practice, 5(1), 1–7. https://doi.org/10.1037/scp0000158

16. Conrad, D., & Kellar-Guenther, Y. (2006). Compassion fatigue, burnout, and compassion satisfaction among colorado child protection workers. Child Abuse & Neglect, 30(10), 1071–1080. https://doi.org/10.1016/j.chiabu.2006.03.009

17. Hall, T. W. (1997). The personal functioning of pastors: A review of empirical research with implications for the care of pastors. Rosemead School of Psychology.

18. Hendron, J. A., Irving, P., & Taylor, B. (2011). The unseen cost: A discussion of the secondary traumatization experience of the clergy. Pastoral Psychology, 61(2), 221–231. https://doi.org/10.1007/s11089-011-0378-z

19. Trihub, B. L., McMinn, M. R., Buhrow, W. C., Jr., & Johnson, T. F. (2010). Denominational support for clergy mental health. Journal of Psychology and Theology, 38(2), 101–110. https://doi.org/10.1177/009164711003800203

20. Leiter, M.P., & Maslach, C. (2017). Motivation, competence and job burnout. In A.J. Elliot, C.S. Dweck, & D.S. Yeager (Eds.), Handbook of competence and motivation (2nd ed., pp.370-384). The Guilford Press.

21. Bandura, A. (1997). The anatomy of stages of change. American Journal of Health Promotion, 12(1), 8–10. https://doi.org/10.4278/0890-1171-12.1.8

22. Bandura, A. (1977). Self-efficacy: Toward a unifying theory of behavioral change. Psychological Review, 84(2), 191–215. https://doi.org/10.1037/0033-295X.84.2.191

23. Bandura, A. (2002). Social cognitive theory in cultural context. Applied Psychology, 51(2), 269–290. https://doi.org/10.1111/1464-0597.00092

24. Bandura, A. (1977). Self-efficacy: Toward a unifying theory of behavioral change. Psychological Review, 84(2), 191–215. https://doi.org/10.1037/0033-295X.84.2.191

25. Bandura, A. (1977). Self-efficacy: Toward a unifying theory of behavioral change. Psychological Review, 84(2), 191–215. https://doi.org/10.1037/0033-295X.84.2.191

"Our story may have any
number of endings, but
its start is a singular
choice we make today."

- Faisal Khosa

# 9

# FINAL CONVERSATION

Church leaders and members are responsible for understanding a pastor's work. The members and leaders should be aware of the expectations, roles, priorities, decisions, and personal time necessary for a pastor not to burn out and function at the highest capacity as a leader in their church.

In the article "Pastoral Burnout and the Impact of Personal Spiritual Renewal, Rest-taking, and Support System Practices," the writer acknowl-

It is a perilous journey for some pastors if church leaders and members do not understand the risks associated with pastoring

edges that leading a church comes

with many challenges, and the risk of burnout is high. It is a perilous journey for some pastors if church leaders and members do not understand the risks associated with pastoring, as noted by the authors of the article "The Unseen Cost: A Discussion of the Secondary Traumatization Experience of the clergy." Church members and leaders must work in tandem to produce a spiritual environment that is productive and healthy for both the members and the pastor.

In addition, there needs to be an increase in educational resources for pastors to understand burnout. Pastors are aware of burnout and the need for self-care; however, there needs to be an increased effort to explain the environmental components of pastoring that could lead to burnout. Pastors face constraints (lack of resources or staffing) that may preclude them from specific actions to reduce burnout. Alternative measures must be made available for pastors to reduce burnout that does not require financial resources or remove them from their weekly church responsibilities.

As we look at these solutions for reducing burnout, you are encouraged to sign up for our mailing list. We will provide more training, updated research, and many other tools to assist pastors with navigating burnout. The first portion of the next section will address solutions related to the pastors, and the second will look at the environment. Where applicable, the solutions are linked to the knowledge points from the earlier chapters.

## The Knowledge Points

1. Based on how pastoring has evolved, it is already positioned towards burnout, even without the devil.
(Chapter 2)

2. Burnout happens over time. (Chapter 3)

3. The correct definition and understanding of burnout are essential to addressing it. (Chapter 4)

4. Burnout is due to a combination of environmental and personal factors. (Chapter 5)

5. Not having a plan or process when leading an organization will lead to burnout. (Chapter 5)

6. A lack of control, community, or competency will lead to burnout. The more of these components that are missing, the faster the pastor will find themselves headed to burnout. (Chapter 6)

7. Compassion is a limited resource (Chapter 8)

# Having a correct and accurate understanding of burnout

## (Knowledge Point #3)

It may seem simple or common sense. However, many people are familiar with the buzzword burnout and do not have a concrete understanding of it. Burnout can look like many other conditions. Pastors must be intentional about learning and understanding burnout, or they will be fighting the wrong fights or missing opportunities to reorient themselves related to burnout.

A pastor who has had to bury three members in two weeks, a youth sentenced to jail, a young couple who miscarried, and a key church member in intensive care may feel tired and want to disengage. That person may *not* be burned out. They may be facing compassion fatigue, a result of being overwhelmed. The nine pastors who shared with us each of them had varying definitions of burnout. In the modern church, if I say "prosperity," people will have different thoughts, ideas, scriptures, and examples because we do not have a unified definition of prosperity. Some think it is evil, others think it is unnecessary, and another group does not want to discuss it.

For us, burnout has a precise definition, and we know what causes burnout to occur. Pastors must be clear on burnout and the actions that lead to it. Work is the trigger for burnout, not lack of sleep or not enough prayer. When a person's work exceeds (or restricts) their ability, capacity, and competency for an extended period, they will begin the steps toward burnout. Every pastor will not face or encounter burnout. However, it does not hurt to know what it is. It cannot be stressed enough how important it is for pastors to know what they will face when it comes to burnout.

## Assessment of Roles

### (Knowledge Point #1)

Pastors, as we discussed, have many roles. Here is a reality we did not address in this book: that church size can impact the pastor's roles. If a church has 50 members versus 5,000 members, the pastor usually has more roles in the smaller church. That does not mean the pastor with the 5,000 members will not experience burnout, as the burden and responsibilities differ. All expenses for the 50-member church could be $2,000 monthly, and the payroll for the 5,000-member church could be $20,000 monthly. The intent is not to see who has more or fewer roles. It is to identify the roles and responsibilities and see if they can be delegated, combined, or eliminated.

When it comes to roles, a pastor must be discerning and prayerful. There are some roles that a pastor may be able to delegate. However, fear of letting go or not having support may be one of many reasons why pastors do not delegate responsibilities. The Responsibilities Worksheet asks pastors to consider what parts of the organization they are touching. For example, do you need to see the song list for the praise team? Do you need to be at every meeting? Do you have to run the entire service and assist with auxiliaries on Sunday? Pastors may not be aware that they are adding additional burdens on themselves. The process for addressing burnout is methodical. It is not often quick and requires personal reflection and honesty. There is also an element of faith and trusting God.

## Use of Systems and Technology

Systems are beneficial; again, a church may be unable to leverage specific systems due to cost or the organization's size. Jethro provided Moses with a system for managing the children of Israel. In addition, in the book of Acts, chapter 6, we see this with the Apostles creating a system for managing the church's work and being faithful to the teaching of the Word. Finding ways to filter information, reducing direct contact with all members, and setting quiet times for you as a pastor can reduce burnout. Technology such as video conferencing has become commonplace since the COVID-19 pandemic. It is excellent for meetings, brainstorming sessions, and other endeavors so that you, as a pastor, do not always have to be at the church.

A pastor should ask questions such as: Do we have a working church structure? Who reports to whom? How often is that chain of command broken, and why? When I worked in consulting, my final product never made it to the senior manager without being seen by the team lead or the manager. It was a system. I could talk to the senior manager and get insight from them or the manager, but the product I was working on never made it to the senior manager until it passed through our system. I will admit I bypassed the system once, which did not go well. Systems are vital and help to manage the roles that the pastor possesses. Again, as the pastor thinks about their roles and the systems in their church, they can identify areas where the organization is not functioning correctly. In some cases, there may not be anything that can be done, while another church may be able to adjust the system to mediate these issues.

# Control, Community, and Competency Must Be Managed

## (Knowledge Point #6)

These three are together because they are a package. A pastor who manages these areas well can reduce their exposure to burnout.

## Control

Pastors should assess their schedules and find possible ways to reduce ambiguity. Pastors who can reduce ambiguity even by a small margin are doing themselves a great service. Humans do not do well with not knowing. In our walk with God, most of us have a problem following God when we do not know where He is leading us. Ambiguity does not work well for us, and pastors are no different. There will be uncontrollable moments, though a pastor's entire day (or ministry) should not be unpredictable. Remember, control is not the same as being controlling or being a micromanager. The pastors should not be controlling everything to try to have control. Does that make sense? Control means having a general idea of how your day, week, or ministerial actions will unfold.

Control is having boundaries and structures in place to manage unexpected issues and to restrict access to you or your family at certain times. A dam does not stop water from being boisterous or moving around. It stops it from going past a certain point. The front door of your house does not stop the rain from falling or the snow from blowing. It stops those elements from entering your house. Pastors must assess the best way to control their schedule and daily activities. As a bonus, pastors who are micromanagers may not burn out, but they will weary the people whom they lead.

## Community

Community or having a sense of belonging is vital. Humans should not be islands. The need for companionship is seen in Genesis when God said it was not good for Adam to be alone. Pastors cannot carry the weight of ministry alone, and their spouse may or may not be the best person to help them navigate certain parts of the ministry. Note that two or a group of burned-out pastors may not help each other. I say that with caution because sometimes empathy is helpful and depends on the person. So, if you and everyone around you are burned out, a fruitful time of fellowship could morph into a gripe or complaining session. It could also be a place that validates terrible decisions or poor choices.

When people are burnt out, their decision-making is restricted, so again, I am not against pastors who are all facing burnout getting together. However, they should be wise in their conversation to ensure the group does not go in the wrong direction. Alternatively, they should ensure they are gathering with a plan to unpack or reflect on what they have been facing and how to make different choices. The real point is to make sure there is a purpose and a predetermined outcome so that the time together is beneficial.

## Competency

As a pastor, do I have all I need to do what I am trying to do? Our world is changing, and we must be ever-learning. As a pastor, do I have the knowledge, understanding, and training to do what I am asked to do? When my wife and I were preparing to get married, the church had a licensed counselor (a Christian) to do our pre-marital counseling, which was a great experience. The critical point is that the person was a *licensed counselor.* The reason for stressing the "licensed" part is that depending on your church, you may need additional credentials or assistance from qualified members. Other churches have formed partnerships with professionals in their area, and when people bring situations to the pastor, they provide spiritual support, prayer, and encouragement. Then, the pastor will outsource the other parts of the intervention to people with the appropriate credentials, education, or experience to assist those individuals.

When humans do activities, they struggle at or do not do well, it takes a mental toll on them. Finding other people in your church or community who can assist helps move the burden of competency. Pastors have to be honest with themselves in order for them to see the areas that need to be adjusted or changed. In addition, various resources online (paid and free) can assist with budgeting, human resources, organizational structure, and other vital areas in the church. A pastor must assess which path is most beneficial for their church and begin to move in that direction. There is no perfect answer, and every church is different, so a pastor must exercise discernment when looking to build competency. Most churches and pastors do not run into issues with the central part of a church, which is theology and preaching. It is the back office work and the functioning of the church that causes the problems.

## Time of Reflection

## (Knowledge Point #2 and #7)

Pastors need to take time to stop and reflect. Pastors must stop and reflect often. This point cannot be stressed enough.

Burnout happens over time. So, if a pastor is not careful, they will burnout or be past the point of burnout before they realize it. Here is one suggestion for how to approach reflections as a pastor. Again, this is a suggestion, and pastors must determine what will work best for them. At the end of every month, take a few hours to sit down and review the month's events.

During this time of reflection, do not have your phone or any other electronic device that could distract you. Your reflection time should be scheduled, and when you will not be interrupted. The list below is a baseline designed to help pastors see how they could approach reviewing their month. Taking moments like this helps with burnout and assessing how much compassion you have expended. Additional questions can be added, but the pastors should decide on a set of questions and attempt to use the same set of questions for continuity. A complete worksheet is available on the Pastor's Paradox website.

> Pastor's need to take time to stop and reflect

## Monthly Reflection Sheet (Example)

*How many Sermons did I preach?*

*How many counseling sessions did I conduct?*

*How many funerals did I conduct?*

*How much online content did I personally produce (online Bible study, online prayer, Facebook live, IG live, etc.) This should be a rough estimate, so do not look at your phone.*

*Based on adverse church events or emergencies, how often did people break protocol and contact the pastor instead of using the specified point of contact?*

*How many of those issues did I end up handling that the point of contact should have handled?*

*How many times did church work interrupt your actual job (for those who work and pastor)?*

*Were there moments when you took away time from your family or personal relationships for the church? If yes, how many times and why?*

*Have I been consistent in my personal prayer time and devotion? If not, why not?*

Visit the Pastor's Paradox for a complete list. This type of reflection allows the pastor to have a snapshot of their month, and as they continue, they can look back over the year and see how their pastoral journey has been progressing.

# Examining the Environment

## (Knowledge Point #4)

### Partnership as a Solution

Churches can be territorial. Pastors have a right and responsibility to "protect" their members and to ensure they are not being led astray or provided with incorrect doctrine. Pastors and churches still need to operate as the Body of Christ. The Bible says, "We are one body, many members." From an environmental standpoint, some churches are operating outside of their capacity. They are essentially doing too much. The phrase "doing too much" does not mean that a church should not be providing a specific service or activity; rather, for that church to properly deliver that service, it will need some external assistance.

There are often opportunities for collaboration and partnership within the Body of Christ. A church wanted to feed people experiencing homelessness in their city, which is a noble undertaking. The congregation was supportive, and eventually, they started the ministry. The church had to go through several processes and complete paperwork to be able to run the ministry to feed those facing homelessness. Now, a church less than 2 miles away on the same street provides the same service and has been doing it for over five years. The church that just started its homeless outreach ministry modeled its "new" ministry after that other church. Why not speak to that pastor and see if your members can volunteer with them? We must learn to work together if we plan to impact the world. The corporations of the world, even the rivals, work together. In most major industries, the top leaders know each other. In the US, the CEOs of major airlines and car manufacturers know each other. They are rivals, yet they coordinate and lobby for legislation and laws that benefit the industry, not just their company. Think about airlines. We have three alliances: Star Alliance, SkyTeam, and Oneworld.

The alliances exist because, let us say, United does not fly to a specific location, but they are in an alliance, so they connect you with a partner who can get you to your destination. Do you see the power of partnership? Since we know that burnout is a combination of environmental and personal factors, partnership is a tool that can be used to address both areas. As the Body of Christ, we must consider partnership more than individual actions. I agree that there are some differences in doctrine or theology. However, that should not be the biggest concern when helping people experiencing homelessness or conducting an after-school tutoring program. Some pastors are burning out because they are doing more than they can handle and are ignoring the power of partnership. If the church (or organization) you want to partner with says no, ok, but at least ask the question.

## Resources

Lack of resources or the necessary resources will lead to burnout. It is not a question of faith. I am not fighting your faith or telling you not to believe what God can do. However, when God provided guidance in the Bible for undertaking specific projects, the resources were usually not far behind. When God told Nehemiah to rebuild the walls of Jerusalem, the King favored him and provided him with letters to gather the necessary materials to complete the project.

I have seen and found with pastors that churches will undertake endeavors based on what the members desire because our world is consumer-driven (there are research papers on this). Churches have started nurseries or children's ministries without adequate personnel, making every Sunday a struggle to manage the ministry. The question of resources is biblical: "Who of you building a building does not first stop and count the cost?" We have seen pastors (or know pastors) who have taken on building projects with no fundamental structure for securing the finances or making the payments and seen churches struggle for years. Some even lose their buildings, thinking people will come if we build a big building. To reduce burnout, we must be aware of our capacity and resources. The lack of those will weigh heavy on the pastor.

## Environmental Deficiencies

Environmental Deficiencies will not always be easy to see. A pastor's environment is dynamic and changes based on the church. Hence, the pastor must ask questions to see if areas in the environment need to be changed, adjusted, revised, or even eliminated. The reason for elimination goes back to one of the pastors' statements that sometimes pastors do too much. That may sound ridiculous, but we must focus on God's instructions. There is a pastor who does not do any conferences or events. He does Sunday morning service and Bible study and brings in other supplemental teachings as needed. He has not been led to host conferences, and his church is doing well. The church is growing. They have paid off debt and are progressing well in bringing light to a dark world.

## Managing Expectations

As one of our pastors mentioned, people can think that the pastor is godlike. Pastors are human. That is not an excuse for sinful behavior, though it is a reason for preservation. People have different views of what a pastor should be because of television, their personal experience, or what they were told. Pastors should, when necessary, find a way to reiterate and manage expectations. Re-explaining the systems or structures is necessary, especially for newer members.

> People have different views of what a pastor should be because of television, their personal experience, or what they were told

As I prepare to round out this chapter, pastors continue to do an extraordinary job of leading the Body of Christ, and these are areas based on research that tend to plague pastors most and lead to burnout. If a person in your congregation has expectations that you (or the church) cannot meet or exceed what you believe God has shown you, it might be a good time to help that person find a new church home. As you make these adjustments, everyone in your congregation will not like them, which is ok. God forbid, but if you burn out, those people who harassed you will probably leave when the new pastor comes, so save them the trouble, pray for them, and let them leave now if they are still unsatisfied.

# Plans for Change

## (Knowledge Point #5)

Everything in this chapter relates to adjustments, realignment, and reconfiguring how we approach and view ministry from the pastor to the congregation. Here is the problem: some of these changes may not be simple.

Once you use the resources that are made available and determine the changes that need to be made, there must be a plan for making those changes. When repairs are made to ships big and small, they bring them into a dry dock. They lift the ship out of the water and perform the maintenance. In this case, most pastors cannot stop their church. It is a living organism, so they must make adjustments while the "ship" is still in the water. One of the simplest forms of initiating change is using what we call "nudges." Nudges are small suggestions that can be used within an organization to point people in a direction without directly expressing it. Nudges utilize positive reinforcement and indirect suggestions to produce outcomes. In addition, nudges are beneficial because they can use past data to show how inaction in the past led to specific consequences.

An example of a nudge could be a pastor saying, "As was discussed in the member's meeting, adjustments to the order of service will be made in the new year for better continuity." Over the next couple of months, the pastor will mention that changes will be coming and provide a little context each time it is mentioned. Now, when the changes happen, it will not be a big surprise or a sudden one, and people will *usually* accept it more easily. The other way is to say, "As you know, over the past three years, we have seen many pastors burning out and having health issues. If we do not adjust how we are organized as a ministry, we risk burning out the pastor and leaders, which is not an outcome that anybody wants." The nudge is to get people to think about a particular issue or an upcoming change. Again, the pastor can explain why the change will happen and what may happen if they do not enact the change.

For larger projects and organizational changes, other tactics may be necessary. Change models are helpful because if you, as a pastor, are making significant changes to preserve your ability to lead, people will have feelings about the changes. Nobody likes to change, and very few people accept it without some conversation. Nudges are some of the most accessible forms of communicating change that do not need a formal structure, though pastors must ensure they are nudging people in the right direction.

When put into action, these solutions will save many pastors from burnout. Pastors may have heard some of the information shared before, though many pastors are not implementing it. Knowing what burnout is and understanding the effect of the church environment on the pastor is unmatched. It is not enough to know; we have to assist our pastors in performing these actions so they can have longevity in ministry.

There are pastors right now, and even the pastors I interviewed who are young and already facing health concerns related to ministry, directly or indirectly. These steps are guidelines and critical to pastors. The online supplemental materials provide added information to help provide guided instruction for understanding change, providing options for change solutions, and better understanding of the topics discussed in this book.

I encourage pastors to get together, talk, discuss, have a book club, think, and review all that is provided. I will research, speak with more pastors, dive into new findings, and continue providing information to help pastors. I aim for a place where pastors can find resources, information, insight, guidance, and materials related to pastoring and the church without going all over the internet. The information is not prescriptive. It is designed to provide context so pastors can make the best decision for their congregation.  Serving God and burning out, my friends is the Pastor's Paradox.

# Chapter Reflections:

1. What is one concept that had a profound impact on you from reading this book?

2. What is one suggestion, idea, or solution that you want to implement at your church?

3. What is one thing you wish you had known when you first started pastoring?

4. Is there a pastor you could recommend this book to?

# About the Author

*Dr. Byron Washington*

Dr. Byron Washington is a Leadership Strategist and Life Consultant. He has over 15 years of experience as a consultant and has led and managed consulting projects for non-profit organizations, educational institutions, and government agencies. Dr. Washington's expertise includes leadership development, change management, business process improvement, and organizational transformation. He is a former speaker and facilitator at the Shanghai American Centre in Shanghai, China, and the Refuge Academy (a faith-based leadership organization) in Abuja, Nigeria. In addition, he has facilitated workshops and leadership sessions in the Republic of Honduras and the Sultanate of Oman.

Dr. Washington is an ordained minister who has worked with churches in China, Singapore, Nigeria, Oman, and the United States. He is a columnist for The Christian Recorder, an AME Church publication. He hosts "The Leadership Ledge Podcast" and is a published author and youth mentor.

Dr. Washington holds a doctorate in Education in Organizational Change and Leadership from the University of Southern California, a master's degree from Princeton University in Public Policy focusing on International Relations, and a bachelor's degree in Business Administration and Finance from Winston-Salem State University.

www.ingramcontent.com/pod-product-compliance
Lightning Source LLC
Chambersburg PA
CBHW051830150726
47998CB00001B/359